Brief Study of the Ten Commandments

Martin Murphy

Brief Study of the Ten Commandments
Copyright © 2014 by Martin Murphy

Published by: Theocentric Publishing Group
                1069A Main Street
                Chipley, Florida 32428

                http://www.theocentricpublishing.com

All rights reserved. No part of this book may be reproduced or transmitted in any form or by any means without written permission of the author.

Unless other noted Scripture is taken from the New King James Version. Copyright © 1979, 1980, 1982 by Thomas Nelson, Inc. Used by permission. All rights reserved.

Library of Congress Control Number: 2014917739

ISBN 9780991481163

To

Bryan Beyer

A godly man

A friend to students

A scholar to the church

Foreword

The Ten Commandments hold an interesting position in both our nation and in the Church. On the one hand, we cannot deny the commandments have shaped our country's legal system and helped define what living a moral life means. Many churches have them posted, and even government buildings sometimes display them (though often not without political ramifications). On the other hand, few Americans and not nearly enough Christians could likely name half of them, let alone all ten.

Martin Murphy's Brief Study of the Ten Commandments challenges its readers to take the Ten Commandments seriously. God's commands are more than suggestions; they are prescriptive for life. They do not represent some kind of "sheltered" way to live; rather, they proclaim the right way to live. The sovereign God of the universe originally gave them to His people as a reflection of His own holy and righteous character. They represent how God would live if He were on earth; and when God did walk this earth in the person of His Son, the Lord Jesus Christ, He did, in fact, endorse them and live by them.

When God originally gave the Ten Commandments, He prefaced them by saying, "I am the Lord your God, who brought you out of the land of Egypt, out of the house of bondage" (Exodus 20:2). This suggests that although people everywhere can and do find value in observing these commands, their primary intention was to provide God's people guidance in how to live as a redeemed people. How tragic that some Christians today would suggest the Ten Commandments have no validity for the Church. On the contrary, those who submit to God's commands will live in the freedom God offers to all His children.

It is my prayer that Martin Murphy's Brief Study of the Ten Commandments will help you in your spiritual journey.

    Bryan Beyer
    Dean of the College of Arts and Sciences
    Columbia International University, Columbia, SC

Table of Contents

1. The Choice is Yours 1
2. God's Law for Godly Choices 9
3. Knowing Who to Worship 17
4. Choose Godly Worship 25
5. The Law of Reverence 35
6. A Special Day for Worship 43
7. The Law of Authority 53
8. The Value of Life 63
9. The Value of Right Relationships 71
10. The Value of a Sacred Trust 81
11. The Value of Truth 91
12. The Law of Contentment 101
13. Where do we go Now? 109
14. Well Begun is not Enough 119
15. Joseph's Godly Choice 127
16. Natural Law is God's Law 133
17. Choose Spiritual Success 147

1. The Choice is Yours

I have given you a land for which you did not labor, and cities which you did not build, and you dwell in them; you eat of the vineyards and olive groves which you did not plant. Now therefore, fear the LORD, serve Him in sincerity and in truth, and put away the gods which your fathers served on the other side of the River and in Egypt. Serve the LORD! And if it seems evil to you to serve the LORD, choose for yourselves this day whom you will serve, whether the gods which your fathers served that were on the other side of the River, or the gods of the Amorites, in whose land you dwell. But as for me and my house, we will serve the LORD.

Joshua 24:13-15

God created Adam so that Adam was perfect in every way. If Adam made a decision, it was a perfect choice. A perfect rational being has a perfect will. Therefore, Adam's choices had to be perfect. However, Adam chose to rebel against God. It was a choice that affected and will affect every human being. Adam's choice to sin against God changed his will from a perfect state to an imperfect state. All of Adam's progeny inherited the sin nature (Romans 5:12-19). The wrong choice will always lead to suffering, sorrow, and pain.

The corruption of sin affects body and soul. The soul consists of the mind, will, and emotions. The will is the component of the soul that motivates a person to make a decision or to make a choice. Human beings make choices, some from sub-conscious inclinations and some from conscious knowledge. Although the purpose of this book is not to engage in philosophical speculation relative to the will of man, it is necessary to explain the nature of the will. The will is a component of the soul. Jonathan Edwards gave as good of an explanation as any I've found or that I might conceive.

The will (without any metaphysical refining) is plainly, that by which the mind chooses anything. The faculty of the will is that faculty or power of principle of mind by which it is capable of choosing: an act of the will is the same as an act of choosing or choice." He goes on to say "A man never, in any instance, wills anything contrary to his desires, or desires anything contrary to his will. (*Freedom of the Will*, vol. 1, Yale edition, p. 137ff)

The nature of man after the fall is such that decisions or choices are either ungodly or godly choices. Christians have a renewed mind and a will that have the potential to make an ungodly choice or a godly choice. The Apostle Paul explains this unique doctrine. "And do not be conformed to this world, but be transformed by the renewing of your mind, that you may prove what is that good and acceptable and perfect will of God" (Romans 12:2). The will of the old nature is inclined to choose for self; self gratification, self fulfillment, self esteem, self worship, all of which are ungodly. The will of the new nature in Christ is inclined to choose for the love of God; it is a godly choice. The new man in Christ may make an ungodly choice, but he has the Holy Spirit, the Word of God, and the church to help him and show him the godly choice.

The Holy Spirit is "in residence" with the soul of every Christian. The Bible explains it in these terms: "He [Jesus Christ] saved us, through the washing of regeneration and renewing of the Holy Spirit" (Titus 3:5). The joy of salvation provided by the Lord Jesus Christ becomes evident after the Holy Spirit gives the believer a new heart. The heart is also known as the soul of man. The image of Christ is formed on the soul of man and will be completely perfected on the last day. The new creature in Christ will have a new and faithful attitude toward the Word of God until he meets Christ face to face. Godly choices will be evident if the Holy Spirit is "in residence" in the soul of man.

The new man in Christ has the unique ability to believe the Word of God. The confrontation that Jesus had with the Jews recorded in John chapter eight explains the difference between superficial belief and serious belief in the Word of God. After Jesus spoke the Words of life, which is the Word of God, the Bible teaches, "many believed in Him" (John 8:21-30). At the beginning of verse 31 there is a transition from the "many" that apparently sincerely believed to "those" who superficially believed. "Then Jesus said to those Jews who believed Him, 'If you abide in My Word, you are My disciples indeed'" (John 8:31). The confrontation escalates, but Jesus continued, "because I tell the truth, you do not believe Me" (John 8:45). Later in that confrontation the Jews tried to kill Jesus, but they failed. In the end they killed Him by hanging Him on the cross. Some unbelievers simply dismiss the Word and others, when they are confronted with the Word, will militate against it. The Christian believer not only has the Holy Spirit "in residence", he also has the Word of God in his heart to guide him to make godly choices.

Christians have peculiar relationships that regulate behavior in this life. They have civil and social relationships that require choices, but they also have spiritual relationships that require choices. God has appointed the church as the means to give Christians spiritual oversight. The doctrine of the church begins with the understanding that "Christ is the head of the church" and therefore the "church is subject to Christ" (Ephesians 5:23-24). It is the authority of Christ that established evangelists, pastors, and teachers "for the equipping of the saints for the work of ministry for the edifying of the body of Christ" (Ephesians 4:11-12). The elders of the church are designated to be "overseers, to shepherd the church of God which He purchased with His own blood" (Acts 20:28). Making godly choices will be much easier if the elders of the church will make godly choices.

The spiritual government of the church is not merely pragmatic or utilitarian. The government of the church is the source of order and authority for the church to carry out its purpose, mission and ministry. It is for that reason that Christ the giver of the mission to the church has appointed the means to bring the children of God to an understanding of the Word of God. It is well known that the church cannot carry out its purpose, mission, and ministry without God's appointed means. Therefore, Christ appointed elders to rule over His church. These elders or presbyters rule by an ultimate standard which is the Word of God. In *Calvin's Catechism of the Church of Geneva* he asked the question: "is it of importance, then, that there should be a certain order of government established in churches?" The answer was "It is: they cannot otherwise be well managed or duly constituted." The church will be a great aid for making godly choices if she is well managed and duly constituted.

Making godly choices may provoke some professing Christians to turn against you. Paul the apostle apparently had a similar experience. Paul wrote the Corinthian Church and said "some, who think of us as if we walked according to the flesh" (2 Corinthians 10:2). Apparently the effort by Paul's opponents was to make Paul look like a worldly minded man, a man acting according to the standards of this world. The only way to correct this false charge against Paul was to think like God thinks. The apostle told the Corinthians that he came with meekness and gentleness because he was a product of the gospel of Jesus Christ. Our appearance and our actions are a result of what we are. I am a Christian therefore I will act, in some sense and to some degree like Jesus Christ. To put it another way the gospel has changed my soul, my soul has changed my thinking, and my thinking has changed my actions. If the change is real it should lead to making godly choices.

The church and therefore the Christians that constitute the church may be influenced by sophistry and deception. Sophistry is a subtle false argument. It is a form of deception by stealth. All too often Christians make the ungodly choice of being silent when the issue of truth is at stake. Since truth is necessary to make godly choices we will do well to remember that "the church of the living God, [is] the pillar and ground of the truth." John Calvin's commentary on 1 Timothy 3:15 has some insight that is worth quoting at this point.

> Now it [truth] is preserved on earth by the ministry of the Church alone. What a weight, therefore, rests on the

pastors, who have been entrusted with the charge of so inestimable a treasure! By holding out to pastors the greatness of the office, he undoubtedly intended to remind them with what fidelity, industry, and reverence they ought to discharge it. How dreadful is the vengeance that awaits them, if, through their fault, that truth which is the image of the Divine glory, the light of the world, and the salvation of men, shall be allowed to fall! This consideration ought undoubtedly to lead pastors to tremble continually, not to deprive them of all energy, but to excite them to greater vigilance... The reason why the Church is called the "pillar of truth" is that she defends and spreads it by her agency. God does not himself come down from heaven to us, nor does he daily send angels to make known his truth; but he employs pastors, whom he has appointed for that purpose...Accordingly in reference to men, the Church maintains the truth, because by preaching the Church proclaims it, because she keeps it pure and entire, because she transmits it to posterity. And if the instruction of the gospel be not proclaimed, if there are no godly ministers who, by their preaching, rescue truth from darkness and forgetfulness, instantly falsehoods, errors, impostures, superstitions, and every kind of corruption, will reign. In short, silence in the Church is the banishment and crushing of the truth. (*Calvin's Commentary*, 1 Timothy 3:15)

Pastors and teachers in the church have the awesome responsibility to preach and teach the truth as it is found in the whole counsel of God. Christians ought to be taught not to use language like "I feel" or "I believe" without reference to the whole counsel of God. Every verse in the Bible must be considered in this noble task. Mimic the Bereans; search the Scriptures daily to find the truth in the Word of God (Acts 17:11).

The Bible uses the expression "according to the flesh" in some cases to refer to the physical presence of Christians living in this world, but not living according to the patterns of this world.

While you are in this world you may live "according to the flesh" which is likely to incline you to make ungodly choices. It is certainly wise to consider your present limitations, because they will affect your ability to make choices. We know that "the god of this world has blinded the minds of the unbelieving" (2 Corinthians 4:4), but he also will try to deceive the elect (Matthew 24:24). God's truth gets to the heart through the head and that is why Satan will try to blind the understanding so that one cannot judge rightly throwing him or her into confusion. Satan will use every conceivable trick to confuse the truth. We identify at least five major areas that may lead the unsuspecting Christian into confusion that will result in making ungodly choices.

- Eloquent speech derived from sophistic arguments.
- Powerful and persuasive propaganda distributed by professing church leaders.
- Charismatic personalities from every branch of the Christian church.
- Managerial madness in the church.
- The therapeutic thrust in the church.

These strongholds can be defeated if pastors and teachers use God appointed weapons. Paul explains to the church that "the weapons of our warfare are not carnal but mighty in God for pulling down strongholds, casting down arguments and every high thing that exalts itself against the knowledge of God, bringing every thought into captivity to the obedience of Christ" (2 Corinthians 10:4-5).

Christians who are empowered by the Holy Spirit and equipped with the Word of God will demolish the false arguments that presume to rise up against the gospel of God. It will take serious inquiry into the Word of God to fight the war that is being waged by evil workers against the church of Jesus Christ. Ask God to protect you from such evil workers and empower you to clearly and cogently cast down arguments and bring every thought captive

1. The Choice is Yours

to the Word of God. Christians are commanded to bring every thought captive to the obedience of Christ. That essentially means Christians are commanded to make godly choices.

After the Promised Land was divided among the twelve tribes of Israel Joshua gathered the tribes to Shechem. He gave them a choice to serve the true and living God or to serve false gods. Joshua made his choice. "But as for me and my house, we will serve the LORD" (Joshua 24:15).

The following chapters in this book are divided into two parts. The first part is an exposition of the Ten Commandments. Understanding the Ten Commandments is necessary for one to make godly choices. The final section of this book will examine a brief portion of the biblical narratives that reveal the lives and circumstances of people making godly and ungodly choices.

2. God's Law for Godly Choices

This day the LORD your God commands you to observe these statutes and judgments; therefore you shall be careful to observe them with all your heart and with all your soul. Today you have proclaimed the LORD to be your God, and that you will walk in His ways and keep His statutes, His commandments, and His judgments, and that you will obey His voice. Also today the LORD has proclaimed you to be His special people. Just as He promised you, that you should keep all His commandments, and that He will set you high above all nations which He has made, in praise, in name, and in honor, and that you may be a holy people to the LORD your God, just as He has spoken.

Deuteronomy 26:16-19

The Lord instructed His people to "keep His commandments." Those instructions are given by injunction from God on fifty two different occasions; forty-two in the Old Testament and ten in the New Testament. If you are a disciple of Jesus Christ, then listen to your teacher. "If you love Me, keep my commandments" (John 14:15). Notice the "if" clause because it establishes a condition in the sentence. There are several ways to understand a conditional sentence in the Greek text, the language God originally inspired. In Greek grammar this, "if clause" is called a 3rd class conditional sentence. It implies doubt or indefiniteness relative to the verb which in this case is love. It might be stated this way: "If you love me (and I'm not sure that you do), keep my commandments." The uncertainty only applies to the present, thus the potential for fulfillment in the future. A good example of this is Peter's relationship to Jesus Christ. Peter denied Jesus three times during the trials and tribulations of the crucifixion, but after the resurrection Peter affirmed his love three times.

Keeping the Lord's commandments presuppose the question of ability to do something. For instance, Jesus said, "No one can serve two lords." To put it another way, "No one is able to serve two lords" (Matthew 6:24). The words "can" and "able" are often misused in the English language, but when it comes to the Word of God they must be used correctly. The words "can" or "able" derives from the Greek Word *dunamis* from which we get the word dynamite. It literally means to have power and most often in theological discourse, it refers to innate power to accomplish something.

The Bible must be examined carefully and thoroughly before we make assertions about ones ability to believe and obey, specifically to believe the gospel and obey the law. Antinomianism is a word all Christians should learn and use, because it refers to the classical argument that it is not necessary to keep or obey the moral law of God. It comes from two Greek words *anti* = against and *nomos* = law. Put them together and you have "against the law" and for Christians an antinomian is "against the law of God."

In modern times this view is known as the "Lordship controversy." Taken to its logical end it means that you may have Christ as Savior, but you do not have to accept Him as Lord. Some preachers and teachers such as C. I. Scofield, Lewis Sperry Chafer and more recently Hal Lindsey, were inclined toward the antinomian view. They do recommend virtuous living, but deny the necessity to keep the moral law, commonly called the Ten Commandments. The vast majority of evangelical preachers, teachers, Bible scholars, and theologians believe that keeping the Ten Commandments is necessary, but not meritorious relative to God's saving grace.

The ability to keep God's commandments is conditioned by the ability to love God. It is a theological axiom that love precedes obedience. Ability does not merely refer to an intellectual concept called love, but rather ability refers to an inward passion that drives a person to love the Lord our God.

Denial of sin is rampant in the church because the church has too long distorted the relationship of the law to the gospel. Dr. Thornwell stated is best when he said, "A law without a sanction is no law, and a sanction unexpected is no sanction" (*The Collected Writings of James Henley Thornwell, Theological and Ethical*, Vol. 2, p. 378).

2. God's Law for Godly Choices

The story is told of a Sunday School superintendent who became concerned when one particular class failed to have any offering for several weeks. The offering plate was placed outside the door each week, but the treasurer did not receive any money. It was discovered that a boy in the department was taking the money. Several weeks before this event, the boy had been recognized for outstanding Bible memory and for being able to quote the Ten Commandments. When he was confronted he did not see any relation between the Ten Commandments and his little act of treason. Maybe he attended a church that taught antinomianism. Knowing the Law of God does not give one the ability to keep the law of God. Knowing words does not necessarily mean that one describes reality with words.

There is so much misunderstanding about God's Law and its application to the human race. There is considerable discussion in every sector about moral behavior, ethics, and lawlessness.

In a survey by the authors of *The Day America Told the Truth* the commandments that people live by should cause alarm and awakening to the truth about God's law. Those surveyed said:

- I don't see the point in observing the Sabbath (77%).
- I will steal from those who won't miss it (74%).
- I will lie when it suits me, if it doesn't cause any real damage (64%).
- I will cheat on my spouse given the fact that he or she will do the same to me (53%).

The church is to blame for such behavior among professing Christians to a certain degree. Sermons dealing with the full nature of the law of God have been absent from many pulpits in this country for over a century.

The gross abuse came with the introduction of anti-intellectualism, fundamentalism, and the liberal social agenda. All of this abuse came as a result of uneducated and unconverted ministers preaching the typical sermon that can be summed up in these words. "God wants you to be good and do good, give to the church, and do not listen to anyone except me."

For too long many preachers have used their own relative humanistic standards, rather than the biblical standards for Christian ethics. They may suppress the eternal will of God, or they may simply rebel against God's Law.

The law of God often referred to as "the Law" has a variety of different meanings in Scripture. God's law is most often understood as the moral law; commonly called the Ten Commandments. The Levitical laws regulated worship in anticipation of the priestly office of Jesus Christ. The judicial case laws prescribed the punishment for violations of the moral law. The Ten Commandments summarize of all God's precepts, ordinances, statutes, decrees and laws.

The Christian church has found three purposes for God's law, commonly known as, civil, theological, and moral.

First – The civil use of the law: The law of God will restrain sin even among those who are not yet believers. The law is like a bridle that keeps them from turning down the path of utter destruction. Romans 2:14, 15 – "for when Gentiles, who do not have the law, by nature do the things in the law, these, although not having the law, are a law to themselves, who show the work of the law written in their hearts, their conscience also bearing witness, and between themselves their thoughts accusing or else excusing them... ."

Second – The theological use of the law: The law of God convicts men of their inability to keep the law and thus drives them to Christ. Galatians 3:24 – "The law was our tutor to bring us to Christ, that we might be justified by faith."

Third – The moral use of the law is more specifically for believers. Deuteronomy 26:18 – "Also today the LORD has proclaimed you to be His special people, just as He promised you, that you should keep all His commandments... ."

2. God's Law for Godly Choices

The third use of the law is the Christian's guide to making godly choices. John Calvin left us with these words. "The third and principle use, which pertains more closely to the proper purpose of the law, finds its place among believers in whose hearts the Spirit of God already lives and reigns" (*Institutes of the Christian Religion*, vol. 1, p. 360).

The third use of the law of God will instruct Christians so that they will make progress toward a genuine knowledge of the divine will. The third use of the law not only instructs, but also calls Christians to avail themselves of the benefits of the law. God's law is a rule of life for believers.

God's law is for God's people, because they alone can keep the law of God so that it is pleasing to God Himself.

It is true that Christians have not fulfilled all the law as a moral being, but God reckons them or accounts them as having performed the whole law in a forensic sense and therefore declared clean by the blood of Jesus Christ. It is through the righteousness of Christ that Christians find grace in the law.

It is the grace of the law that shines forth in the Bible. Christians and only Christians understand the grace of God's law. Therefore, Christians are in a unique relation to the law.

First, God's law is unique because, the burden to keep the law is ever before Christians. "God commands you to observe these statutes and judgments" (Deuteronomy 26:16). This Old Testament reference applied to all the divine laws set forth in God's covenant with His people including all the ceremonial and judicial laws. His divine law is fully explained in the previous chapters of the book of Deuteronomy. However, God's covenant people are not commanded to obey Moses, but rather to obey God. The responsibility to keep God's divine law was a condition to the covenant which God made with His people.

The Lord instructs His people to obey, love, and repent with all the heart and with all the soul.

- Deuteronomy 30:2 - obey God with all your heart and all your soul.

- Deuteronomy 30:6 - love the Lord with all your heart and all your soul.
- Deuteronomy 30:10 - turn to the Lord with all your heart and all your soul.

Do you see the predicament for Christians? We talk and sing about obeying God, but can we do it with all our heart and soul? We talk and sing about loving Jesus, but are we able to love Jesus with all our heart and soul? Can we turn to the Lord with all our heart and soul? Can we make godly choices? Obedience to God and love for God will incline the heart to turn to God. These are necessary to make godly choices.

The Old Testament church made this promise. "Today you have proclaimed the Lord to be your God, and that you will walk in His ways and keep His statutes, His commandments, and His judgments, and that you will obey His voice" (Deuteronomy 26:17). Christians today make similar promises when they join the church. They promise to live as a follower of Christ. They promise to be faithful in the performance of their Christian duties. They promise to seek the peace, purity and prosperity of the church. Some are promise keepers and many are promise breakers.

When we promise to keep God's divine law, we engage the mind, the emotions and the will. Your mind interprets God's Word, so you will understand God's law. Your will compels you to lovingly keep God's law. Your emotions passionately affirm the inward promise by your outward actions. So it is said that Christians walk in His ways, keep His commandments, and obey His voice.

Believers sense the burden to keep the law and so they promise to keep the law because in it they find grace. Christians find grace in the law because they are God's peculiar people. God's people are the most cherished of all people. Remember what Calvin said, "the proper purpose of the law finds its place among believers in whose hearts the Spirit of God already lives and reigns."

God's people are special people and that is the reason they should keep His commandments.

2. God's Law for Godly Choices

Unbelievers seek grace in the law and never find it, but the believer is a special person and finds joy in keeping God's commandments. Yes, Christians will fail because although sin does not reign in the saint of God, it remains in the saint of God. The difference is the believer finds grace where the unbeliever finds despair and desperation.

God's people are not only cherished, they are consecrated. They are a holy people unto the Lord. They belong to God. The Psalmist expressed it in these terms. "For the Lord has chosen Jacob for Himself, Israel for His special treasure" (Psalm 135:4).

God's people are set apart by the blood of Jesus Christ to keep His commandments and to love His divine law. God's people find joy, gratitude and peace in keeping God's commandments.

When you are faced with making moral choices, remember God's commandments.

3. Knowing Who to Worship

You shall have no other gods before Me.

Exodus 20:3

The most important choice a person will ever make is deciding who to worship. Every rational creature on planet earth must decide to worship false gods or to worship the true God. The Bible has many examples of men and women choosing to worship false gods.

Ahab is one example of a man who chose to worship false gods.

> Now Ahab the son of Omri did evil in the sight of the LORD, more than all who were before him.....he went and served Baal and worshiped him. Then he set up an altar for Baal in the temple of Baal, which he had built in Samaria. And Ahab made a wooden image. Ahab did more to provoke the Lord God of Israel to anger than all the kings of Israel who were before him. (1 Kings 16:30-33)

Elijah confronted Ahab, but the wicked king accused Elijah of being a "troubler of Israel."

> And he answered, "I have not troubled Israel, but you and your father's house have, in that you have forsaken the commandments of the LORD and have followed the Baals" (1 Kings 18:18). Ahab and the prophets of Baal gathered together against Elijah. One question was on the mind and tongue of Elijah for the people of Israel. "How long will you falter between two opinions?" (1 Kings 18:21)

The word "falter" is traced to a Hebrew word that means, "to limp." The word "opinion" comes from a Hebrew word that may also be translated "cleft" which means "divided." The tragedy of life is to be divided between false gods and the true God. The great joy of life is to know who to worship.

Christians will never understand the object of worship, until they understand the doctrine of the first three of the Ten Commandments. The first three commandments are often called the God-first commands, because they deal with the nature and character of God and how Christians are commanded to worship Him.

When the Pharisees asked Jesus "which is the greatest commandment in the law" Jesus responded, "You shall love the Lord your God with all your heart, with all your soul, and with all your mind" (Matthew 22:37). We hear the essence of that command no less than thirteen times in the Bible. The perusal of the corpus of Scripture teaches that the full energy of body and soul is required to love the true and living God. Love of the object of worship, the Lord God almighty, is prerequisite to worship.

The first commandment is the foundation for all the other commandments, so it demands your full attention. In fact the first commandment is the foundation for all religion. The first of the Ten Commandments contains a few words, but what profound, powerful, probing, provocative, and persuasive words.

Who will deny that human beings are not worshipping creatures? Human beings are religious people and religion must have an object to worship. Human beings were created to worship the true God of heaven and earth as He is described in the Bible. However, because of the fall the sinful nature of man is such that self worship dominates the soul. Unbelievers worship the creature rather than the Creator.

The history of the human race is a history of worshipping people. The evidence may be found with the Paul's visit to the philosophers at Athens. It was a place and a people especially given to intellectual stimulation and with it the high culture of the day. Upon arriving in the arena, Paul "stood up in the meeting of the Areopagus" and brought up some of the observations of his tour of Athens. "Men of Athens! I see that in every way you are very religious. For as I walked around and looked carefully at your objects to worship, I even found an altar with this inscription: TO AN UNKNOWN GOD. Now what you worship as something unknown I am going to proclaim to you" (Acts. 17:22-23).

Today scarcely anyone would claim to worship an unknown god, but innumerable are those who worship particular, private, and public gods shaped according to their own imaginations. Christians are not exempt. John Calvin said, "the proper purpose of the law finds its place among believers in whose hearts the Spirit of God already lives and reigns" (*Institutes of the Christian Religion*, 2.10.12).

Christians above all people on earth should take pleasure in the law of God, because it teaches the way of sanctification. Understanding the doctrine of sanctification and the individual Christian growing in sanctification is inseparable from knowing who to worship. Sanctification is the process of being made righteous. The late professor John Murray explained the doctrine of sanctification.

> Sanctification involves the concentration of thought, of interest, of heart, mind, will, and purpose upon the prize of the high calling of God in Christ Jesus and the engagement of our whole being with those means which God has instituted for the attainment of that destination. Sanctification is the sanctification of persons, and persons are not machines; it is the sanctification of persons renewed after the image of God in knowledge, righteousness, and holiness. The prospect it offers is to know even as we are known and to be holy as God is holy" (*Redemption, Accomplished and Applied*, by John Murray, p. 150).

Knowing God's will is necessary to grow in sanctification. God's will is, "You shall have no other gods before me" (Exodus 20:3).

God creates, governs, and judges all men and their actions, yet they find themselves seeking other gods. In what ways do men seek other gods? They seek gods that they can control. Human beings are experts in inventing idols or false gods. All men do not worship the same false gods, but all men are guilty of idolatry.

It is a trifle assertion to claim to be free of this sin. It is innate among rational people, Christians and unbelievers. The sin of idolatry goes deep in the crevices of the soul. Idolatry begins with the first commandment. "You shall have no other gods before Me."

The Bible describes false gods as forsaking the true and living God to espouse any other god. (This is known as "spiritual adultery" which I discuss in depth in chapter eight). Avoid idolatry and you will not have any false gods in the face of the true God. If you have the proper reverence for God you will not fall into idolatry.

Living in this world involves the privilege of engaging with culture. There are all types of institutions which in themselves are not sinful, but they become sinful if they become an object of worship. The *Shema* is the preface necessary to understand this commandment. The *Shema* is a short prayer that reflects God's unique character. "Hear, O Israel: The LORD our God, the LORD is one!" (Deuteronomy 6:4). This brief prayer asserts the reality of God being one God. Attached to the prayer is a command. "You shall love the LORD your God with all your heart, with all your soul, and with all your strength" (Deuteronomy 6:5). Any material object, concept, or institution may compete for your love. There are many of them.

Hobbies may consume so much time and effort that they become an object of worship.

Financial assets may turn into a false god and become a spiritual liability.

Civic clubs often become a substitute for ministry in the church.

Sports events have become objects of worship, even for many professing Christians.

3. Knowing Who to Worship

Clothes, cars, trucks and boats may become the gods of style and prestige.

Food and drink are gods for some people.

Real estate, especially a home, may become a false god.

Entertainment is probably the most prominent false god in America.

The unfaithful church along with tradition, buildings, and false doctrine are the most powerful false gods for the majority of professing Christians. The list of false gods is endless.

But do you know the false god who creates all these false gods? It is the "old man." Sometimes the chief of all false gods is self-esteem, the spark of divinity, the center of creation, or any other psychological, sociological or theological name; however, it still boils down to one thing - self worship. Nebuchadnezzar, the king of Babylon, claimed to be a god to himself. "I am and there is no one else besides me" (Isaiah 47:8-10). It is the same sin that causes professing Christians to worship the Ego.

> I worship my agenda.
> I worship my goals.
> I worship my ideas.
> I worship my position of authority.
> In short I worship myself.

God gave the Israelites the Ten Commandments written in stone. The LORD delivered the "two tablets of stone written with the finger of God" (Deuteronomy 9:10). They are summarized in the *Shema* and the great commandment; The Lord is one (Deuteronomy 6:4-5). The distinction is the singularity of God. There is a great difference between singularity and plurality. The end result of plurality is pluralism. The Israelites were about to enter the land of Canaan. It was the land of deistic pluralism; the land of many gods. The application is as contemporary as the daily newspaper. God commands His people to worship one God, the true and living God of heaven and earth. Self-centered worship is the great enemy to God-centered worship. Self-centered worship is the home of many gods. Self-centered worship will suppress spiritual growth and may reflect the lack of union and communion with the true object of worship, the Lord God almighty.

Many of us wish that semantic categories were not necessary in the science of interpretation, but because of our fallen estate, we cannot think in ultimate and absolute terms. We tend to place conditions on ultimate and absolute propositions. God gave an ultimate and absolute command: "You shall have no other gods before me." Does that also mean, "you shall have some gods before me or may we have some gods under certain conditions?" If we think in those categories then we change the ultimate to the proximate and we change the absolute to the conditional. Those changes are in the wrong direction. When we think of God we must always move from the proximate to the ultimate. Our minds must shift from the conditional to the absolute. Anything less means moving from the true God to false gods. Jesus said, "No one can serve two masters; for either he will hate the one and love the other, or else he will be loyal to the one and despise the other. You cannot serve God and mammon" (Matthew 6:24). Christ redeemed His people to love the true God and hate all false gods.

The true and living God must be the height of your adoration and trust. Christians must recognize His greatness as the creator, sustainer, and redeemer. They must recognize the sovereign, almighty, eternal, triune God. Make this personal; in order to recognize Him you must know Him.

> Know Him in His attributes.
> Know Him in His holiness.
> Know Him in His grace and mercy.
> Know Him in his faithfulness.
> Know Him in His Son, the Lord Jesus Christ.

3. Knowing Who to Worship

To say that you know and love God is to say that you are in a covenant relationship with Him. When Christians renew their covenant relationship with God in the sacrament of the Lord's Supper, they must come to the table with God alone; not with any other gods. The Lord will not meet Christians if they bring other gods with them. Do you rely on God's power as your Creator and Sustainer? Do you trust his love like a father's love to his child?

Then how much more should you put aside your false gods and find greater pleasure in the true and living God. The first commandment primarily teaches Christians that they must worship and that they must worship the one and only true and living God. It shows Christians the object of true worship. Infinite perfection should be the object of worship. Who would want to worship temporary and imperfect objects and therefore deify defective objects? Would you purchase a defective washing machine or a bent up car with a bad engine? No! So why store up false gods? They are defective! Get rid of them. Get the real thing.

Knowing who to worship is the supreme objective in this life. Knowing who to worship is necessary to understand the purpose of this life.

4. Choose Godly Worship

You shall not make for yourself a carved image – any likeness of anything that is in heaven above, or that is in the earth beneath, or that is in the water under the earth; you shall not bow down to them nor serve them. For I, the LORD your God, am a jealous God, visiting the iniquity of the fathers upon the children to the third and fourth generations of those who hate Me, but show mercy to thousands, to those who love Me and keep My commandments.
                                                                Exodus 20:4-6

The law of God is given specifically for God's people and as Calvin says, "the proper purpose of the law finds its place among believers in whose hearts the Spirit of God already lives and reigns." Calvin said that because believers love the law of God (Psalm 119:97).

If Christians expect to understand the second commandment, they must remember that the first commandment is foundational to all the other commandments. It tells God's covenant people who to worship. The preface to the first commandment declares the sovereignty of God. "I am the LORD your God, who brought you out of the land of Egypt, out of the house of bondage" (Exodus 20:2).

The redemptive expression of God's triune character is found in the first chapter of Ephesians.

> God chose us in Jesus Christ before the foundation of the world and in Christ we have obtained an inheritance, being predestined according to the purpose of God who works all things according to the counsel of His will and you were sealed with the Holy Spirit of promise to the praise of God's glory. (See Ephesians 1:4-14)

The glory of the triune God is the reason for godly worship. Ungodly worship denies the excellent character of the triune God.

If God is sovereign and redeems His people from bondage then why do so many not worship the true and living God? The answer is they are without Christ. As Christ said to the woman at the well at Samaria, "you worship that which you do not know" (John 4:22).

The Samaritans were not worshiping an unknown God as the Athenians, but they worshipped according to their own imaginations. The Samaritans rejected the prophetical and poetical books of the Old Testament therefore drastically reducing their understanding of the true and living God. They, like many Christians today, failed to consult the whole counsel of God. The only way to know who to worship is by having the spiritual eyes opened. It is the renewing of the mind, emotions and will that allows the believer to worship the true and living God.

The second commandment follows from the first in that it tells Christians how to worship the true and living God. The first commandment prohibits worship to false gods. The second commandment commands Christians not to worship the true God in a false manner.

God commands worship, service and obedience according to the pleasure of His good will. In fact God said, "Whatever I command you, you shall be careful to do; you shall not add to nor take away from it" (Deuteronomy 12:32). The professing believer may think or feel that God will like some part of worship even if God did not command it. The collective doctrine found in the corpus of Scripture is clear. Worship is not acceptable to God, unless God commands it in the Word of God. At the risk of sounding redundant, it must be repeated. The way to know God's will relative to worship, service, and obedience is from the Word of God; all of it, not just a verse or two, but take into account the whole counsel of God.

The Bible makes it very clear that we must not worship any idols or the likeness of any object in creation.

> Take careful heed to yourselves, for you saw no form when the Lord spoke to you at Horeb out of the midst of the fire, lest you act corruptly and make for yourselves a carved

4. Choose Godly Worship

image in the form of any figure; the likeness of male or female, the likeness of any animal that is on the earth or the likeness of any winged bird that flies in the air, the likeness of any thing that creeps on the ground or the likeness of any fish that is in the water beneath the earth" (Deuteronomy 4:15-18).

Moses spoke those words to warn the children of God relative to false worship, both the object of worship and the manner of worship.

The Old Testament church understood how to worship because they had been taught the statues and judgments commanded by God (Deuteronomy 4:14). The eternal principle is very simple. The people of God have to worship God the way He commands them to and not the way they want to worship.

What is worship? The 18th century English puritan, Dr. Thomas Ridgeley, gave a godly and biblical definition of the manner of worship. "Religious worship is that whereby we address ourselves to God, as a God of infinite perfection."

It is possible for Christians to offer worship to the God of infinite perfection if they obey God's commandments and worship Him in spirit and truth. God is a spiritual being and Christians must conceive of God spiritually. God is infinite, eternal, and unchangeable. He is the God of absolute holiness on hand and absolute justice on the other. Christians must worship God without any physical considerations or the use of any images. Spiritual worship honors God and invigorates the soul of man.

The joy of choosing godly worship is a great privilege, but choosing ungodly worship is useless idolatry. "Those who make an image, all of them are useless, and their precious things shall not profit" (Isaiah 44:9). The apostle Paul called idolatry a work of the flesh (Galatians 5:20). The warning to the New Testament church is to "flee from idolatry" (1 Corinthians 10:14).

Christian worship drifts into idolatry because Christians in general and church leaders in particular do not take seriously the warnings from the full counsel of God. For some reason contemporary Christianity simply dismisses the words and warnings from God. Maybe they think idolatry is a reference to false gods made of wood or metal in far away places. Idolatry is nothing less than the worship of human forms and institutions. Idolatry turns the spiritual in the physical and the truth into a lie. When God told the church in the Old Testament not to make an idol or any likeness of anything that is in heaven or earth, God was speaking to the church of all ages.

The church must not seek to invent new ways to worship, for to do so will surely create human centered worship which is forbidden.

Christians must be very careful to worship the true God in the manner in which He has prescribed in His Word. God is a jealous God. He protects His name for His special people. He has a special love for them. God is jealous because He is sovereign and has the right to rule over His creatures. The unregenerate man is like a spiritual adulterer who is filthy and defiled, because of his love of idols. God removes all the filth and turns the unregenerate man into a virgin. Then the regenerate man or woman loves God above all else. If God can turn a sin stained adulterer into a virgin, God has every right to be jealous.

God is not merely a capricious jealous God; He is a sovereign God. Since God is sovereign the redeemed worshipper does not have to try to figure out what God wants. The duty of the redeemed worshipper is to worship God according to God's commandments and no other way.

God appoints pastors to lead the congregation in public collective worship. Since the pastor and the congregation have a sinful heart, idolatry will raise its ugly head. It is easy to make man the center of worship. If man is the center of worship, the preacher will be loved or hated. The singing will be good or bad. The organ will be either too loud or the choir is not loud enough. I didn't like that sermon. I didn't like that song. It is easy to make *self* the center of worship.

"I was expecting something better", says the professing Christian. Christians cannot expect to put God at the center of worship if "self" is in the way. If "I" wants to be the center of worship, that is the great sin of idolatry, in its worst form.

Is entertainment more important than understanding God's nature and character? That is false worship and a violation of the second commandment. Does the worshipper desire light-hearted, humorous, anecdotal sermons over sermons that reveal sin on one hand and the majesty of God on the other? It may be translated to mean, "I like a short, simple fifteen minute sermon." That is false worship and a violation of the second commandment. Is the wisdom of the preacher preferred rather than the wisdom of God? That is false worship and a violation of the second commandment.

When Amos confronted the false worship in his day, God said, "I hate, I despise your religious feasts; I cannot stand your assemblies" (Amos 5:21). God tried to warn the Old Testament church of the coming judgment. God said that to Old Testament Israel, the professing believers in that day. After nearly 2700 years God still means what He said about worship. Hosea's prophecy resounds God's warnings in Scripture. "I desire mercy, not sacrifice, and acknowledgment of God rather than burnt offerings" (Hosea 6:6). False worship is wrong whether it is outward or from the heart. Outward worship is worthless, if you despise the true worship of God in the heart.

Generational continuity is necessary to maintain true worship to the true God in the manner in which He has prescribed in His Word. If the children follow the false worship of the previous generation, it will become exponentially worse (Exodus 20:5). If one generation violates the second commandment, God promises to punish the generations to come. It appears from this text that it is a special sin. It is the hereditary effect of your sin on your children. The sin of one generation is devolved to the next generation by generational continuity. For instance, you teach your children perverse forms of worship. Later in life they fail to consult the Word of God and pass principles of false worship their children. Each generation continues in the morass of error, because they did not consult the Word of God. Then God visits future generations with his anger and wrath. Every Christian ought to stop and think for a moment and ask this question. Why are so many evangelicals not making godly choices? It is possible that God is fulfilling His promise by "visiting the iniquity of the fathers upon the children to the third and fourth generations of those who hate me" (Exodus 20:5). For the sake of the next generation choose godly worship and be careful to worship the true God in the true manner in which He has prescribed in His Word. According to the words from the mouth of God, violation of the second commandment reflects hatred for God. This is demonstrated several different ways:

> Professing Christians who believe and act contrary to God's expressed will.

> Professing believers, who hate God's children, hate the Father.

> Then there are those who hate God's truth in spite of the evidence.

God's Word prescribes a particular way to worship, therefore any other way becomes offensive to God and consequences will follow. Nadab and Abihu, the sons of Aaron, were put to death because they offered worship to God that He had not commanded (Leviticus 10:1). Some Christians believe this was an Old Testament regulation and does not apply to New Testament Christians. Although some of the Levitical and Judicial case laws have either expired or been abrogated, the general equity and principles found in the text are still applicable today. To dismiss the full counsel of God is to dismiss some of the words that came from the mouth of God. There is not one word that came from the mouth of the sovereign God that is considered useless.

Another example of God's punishment to those who worship false gods is found in Deuteronomy chapter thirteen.

> If your brother, the son of your mother, your son or your daughter, the wife of your bosom, or your friend who is as

> your own soul, secretly entices you, saying, 'Let us go and serve other gods,' which you have not known, neither you nor you fathers, of the gods of the people which are all around you, near to you or far off from you, from one end of the earth to the other end of the earth, you shall not consent to him or listen to him, nor shall your eye pity him, nor shall you spare him or conceal him; but you shall kill him; our hand shall be first against him to put him to death, and afterward the hand of all the people. And you shall stone him with stones until he dies, because he sought to entice you away from the LORD your God, who brought you out of the land of Egypt, from the house of bondage. (Deuteronomy 13:6-11)

If one is tempted to say that portion of God's Word refers to the God of the Old Testament, one should quickly repent and remember that God is one (Deuteronomy 6:5). Then what could this text mean to the New Testament Christian? Jesus said, "whoever causes one of these little ones who believe in Me to stumble, it would be better for him if a millstone were hung around his neck and were thrown into the sea" (Mark 9:42).

False worship springs forth from a sinful heart. Then it devolves from one generation to the next. Finally true worship is forgotten. The history of worship in the nation of Israel is an example of choosing ungodly worship. After Solomon had built the Temple, God appeared to Solomon.

> And the LORD said to him: "I have heard your prayer and your supplication that you have made before Me; I have consecrated this house [the Temple in Jerusalem] which you have built to put My name there forever, and My eyes and My heart will be there perpetually. Now if you walk before Me as your father David walked, in integrity of heart and uprightness, to do all that I have commanded you, and if you keep My statutes and My judgments, then I will establish the throne of your kingdom over Israel forever, as I

promised David your father, saying, You shall not fail to have a man on the throne of Israel. But if you or your sons at all turn from following Me, and do not keep My commandments and My statutes which I have set before you, but go and serve other gods and worship them, then I will cut off Israel from the land which I have given them; and this house which I have consecrated for My name I will cast out of My sight." (1 Kings 9:4-7)

God warned Solomon to not serve other gods and worship them or there would be consequences (circa 1000 B.C.). About 400 years later false worship had multiplied to the point that God would soon keep his promise to cast them out of His sight. The Word of the LORD came to Jeremiah saying, "But where are the gods that you have made for yourselves? Let them arise, if they can save you in the time of your trouble; For according to the number of your cities are your gods, O Judah" (Jeremiah 2:28). There were as many false gods as there were cities in Judah. In the Old Testament we find that false prophets often out number the prophets of God. There is no reason to believe the church is better off today than in the days of Elijah, Isaiah, or Jeremiah.

Choosing godly worship pleases God. "He shows mercy to those who love Him and keep His commandments" (Exodus 20:6). If Christians worship God the way He commands them to worship Him, they may experience the mercy, love and goodness of God. The general biblical principles are to worship God in spirit and truth, for His glory, decently and in order. The Bible provides ample evidence for Christians to know how to worship God in spirit and truth, for His glory, with reverence and adoration. Consulting the **whole counsel of God**, I conclude that God commands the following for collective worship by a congregation of God's people.

1. Reading of Scripture
2. Preaching of the Word
3. Prayer

4. Sacraments
5. Confession of sin and faith
6. Singing of Psalms and hymns
7. Gathering the offerings
8. The benediction

All of these elements of worship are to exalt God the Father, God the Son and God the Holy Spirit.

Jesus Christ has redeemed his people for the express purpose of exalting Him as the fountainhead of religious worship. It is hard to find the words to explain just how serious God takes the second commandment. The Lord Jesus Christ said, "These people draw near to Me with their mouth and honor Me with their lips but their heart is far from Me and in vain they worship me teaching as doctrines the commandments of men" (Matthew 15:8-9).

Why did Jesus say these things? The religious leaders of His day asked Him the question, "Why do Your disciples transgress the tradition of the elders?" (Matthew 15:2). The answer was that the tradition was not in agreement with the commandments of God. They were worshipping, allegedly the true God in the wrong manner. If something takes place in worship that God has not commanded in the Word of God, then it is false worship. All worship has an object; therefore the object of false worship is a false god. If professing believers could grasp the import, the weight, the significance of the words of our Lord Jesus Christ, true revival would break out in every congregation of God's people.

On the appointed time on the Sabbath the congregation assembles to worship according to God's Word. That is outward worship. What really counts is how you worship God inwardly. It is called heart worship. It requires the right heart attitude toward the elements of worship that are conducted outwardly. It is a great blessing to God's people when they worship the true and living God according to His commandments.

5. The Law of Reverence

You shall not take the name of the LORD your God in vain, for the LORD will not hold him guiltless who takes His name in vain.
Exodus 20:7

Making wise choices ought to be the desire of every Christian. How do we go about making wise choices? Joshua told the people of God over 3000 years ago to, "Choose for yourselves this day whom you will serve" (Joshua 24:15). You will make a wise choice if you choose to serve the one true and living almighty, sovereign God. You will make a wise choice if you choose to worship the true God according to His revealed will. You will make a wise choice if you choose to revere him above all other created beings or objects. To put it another way, choose the law of reverence.

God spoke to His people most often through men or angels. For example, Paul the Apostle wrote to the Corinthian church through his own personality. Although inspired by God, the personality of the author is obvious. The Ten Commandments came directly from the mouth of God and Scripture even mentions that the Ten Commandments were "written with the finger of God" (Exodus 31:18). The word "written" from that text is from the Hebrew word *kathab* which the *New American Standard Bible* translates "inscribed" in Exodus 39:30. An inscription engraved on a precious metal or stone, reflects the permanent nature of the writing. The finger of God does not mean God took the form of human flesh. The finger of God is a figure of speech that certainly implies the immediate action of God without the human personality being involved.

The fact that God spoke and wrote the Ten Commandments does not make them any more binding than the rest of Scripture, but it does reflect the gracious hand of God in giving His people the law of God.

The law of God is sufficient to warn and condemn sinners whether the law is expressly natural or through special revelation. <u>Every Christian ought to remember every fleeting moment that every human being that has lived, now lives, or ever will live has the law of God written on the heart.</u> The previous sentence was underlined to stress that the law is written on the heart because much of western evangelicalism has ignored the doctrine of natural law (Romans 2:14-16). However, the Ten Commandments found in the Word of God are uniquely given by God to His people for their own good.

The first three commandments are called the God first commands. They direct our attention to God and His personality. Notice that God moves from the general to the particular. The First Commandment calls attention to God's existence, which is a more general truth than the specificity which follows it. The second commandment is an injunction to choose godly worship.

The third Commandment is more specific although still closely connected with the first two. The third commandment is the law of reverence. It commands Christians to revere God's name above all other names. The biblical concept of reverence belongs especially to God. Due reverence for God's name is a positive comprehensive command.

In Haggai's prophecy a remnant of God's people came out of captivity and returned to Jerusalem to rebuild the temple. When the people gathered together, the *New King James Version* explains "the people feared the presence of the Lord" (Haggai 1:12). The *New American Standard Bible* translation is slightly different: "The people show reverence for the Lord." Fear and reverence may be interchangeable if the words are properly understood within the biblical context. For the children of God, the fear of God is wholesome. It is reverence in the presence of God. For the enemies of God, fear is an unhealthy disposition that creates all kinds of phobia. A phobia is an abnormal fear or dread of something. There are hundreds of known and labeled abnormal fears that people have. They range from *claustrophobia*, a fear of confined spaces, to *theophobia*, a fear of God. My phobia is that there is too much *bibliophobia*, a fear of the Bible, or what the Bible teaches.

Improper fear, especially the fear of God is because of the sinfulness of man and being indisposed to the law of God. It leads to an improper reverence of self. In reality people like their name revered but show little reverence for God's name.

I'm not particularly fond of the title "reverend," because it means to revere and traced to its Latin root it means to worship. The word reverend comes from the same Latin word as the word venerate. The Roman Catholic Church practices the "veneration of saints." Although the church denies that it means the worship of saints, it does revere the saints even to the degree that they are canonized by the church.

It seems that Christians find it easy to entertain the idea that God's name may be taken lightly. God's name reflects the sanctity of God's reputation. It is particularly important to understand the names of God. If Christians do not understand the names of God, they will not understand His nature, character, or His will.

So often Christians misuse and abuse God's name because of ignorance. God's names reflect His nature and character. Ignorance of God's supreme wisdom, infinite power, justice and truth is often the case when God's names are not understood. Understanding the law of reverence is necessary to avoid false worship.

The logic of the first three commandments is so obvious. The proper use of the name of God will lead to true worship and true worship will lead to the only true and living God. We are all familiar with Isaiah 52:7 where God is revered as the sovereign king of salvation. But are we familiar with the previous verses? In verse five God says, "My name is blasphemed continually every day." The word blasphemed means to "treat with contempt." The unbelieving nations did not treat God's name with respect. Then in verse six God says, "Therefore My people shall know my name."

The saving grace of God belongs to those who know His name. "The name of the Lord is a strong tower; The righteous run to it and are safe" (Proverbs 18:10).

Each Hebrew or Greek word that is translated God or Lord in the Bible, expresses something different about His nature and character. A few examples are:

Jehovah = Lord = His self existence
El = God = His might and power
Elohim = God = Object of adoration, fear, reverence
Elyon = God = Most High

The names for the second person of Trinity:
Jesus = Joshua = Savior = save from sins
Christ = Messiah = Anointed one = deliverer
Lord = Jehovah = self existence

Christians may say "the name above all names is Jesus" and quote Philippians 2:9-10, but they do not finish the sentence. This text is very important because it describes God's proper name and how His children must use His name. "Therefore God also has highly exalted Him and given Him the name which is above every name, that at the name of Jesus every knee should bow, of those in heaven and of those on earth and of those under the earth and that every tongue should confess that Jesus Christ is Lord, to the glory of God the Father" (Philippians 2:9-11). The name that is above all names is LORD. God the Father and God the Son both have the same name. The name is LORD. The Bible also refers to the third person of the trinity as the Spirit of the LORD.

Jesus Christ as a name is specifically concerned with the salvation of God's elect. Lord as a name is the highest title known to human language especially the Hebrew, Greek, and English language. At the proper time every created being will bow before the Lord. One may not give reverence to God's name now, but the time will come when reverence will have its place.

Christians should approach the passage in Exodus looking for the freshness that comes from God's word. The text says the name of the Lord must not be used in vain. "You shall not take the name of the Lord in vain" (Exodus 20:7). The word "vain" comes

5. The Law of Reverence

from a Hebrew word that essentially means "emptiness" or "worthlessness".

God commanded Judah to stop bringing worthless (or vain) sacrifices to the worship service (Isaiah 1:13). Now to restate the third commandment; You shall not take the name of the Lord your God in a worthless manner. Worth implies value and there is an eternal value in God's name. When one neglects to call upon the name of the Lord according to Scripture, it reflects a lack of interest in God's name, therefore making God's name worthless.

The commandment certainly teaches that we must not use or implicate the names of the LORD in vulgar everyday language in a manner that does not show respect, reverence and worth to God's name. People may say "Oh my God" or "Oh my Lord" in a disrespectful manner and without any thought of the nature and character of the Person that owns the name. To have God on your tongue and not on your heart is blasphemy and a sin against God according to the third Commandment.

This commandment teaches Christians that if they profess God's name they must live by His name. If their profession of faith is contrary to their everyday lives, they break the third commandment. Jesus gave a solemn warning in this regard.

> "Beware of false prophets, who come to you in sheep's clothing, but inwardly they are ravenous wolves. You will know them by their fruits. Do men gather grapes from thornbushes or figs from thistles? Even so, every good tree bears good fruit, but a bad tree bears bad fruit. A good tree cannot bear bad fruit, nor can a bad tree bear good fruit. Every tree that does not bear good fruit is cut down and thrown into the fire. Therefore by their fruits you will know them. Not everyone who says to Me, 'Lord, Lord,' shall enter the kingdom of heaven, but he who does the will of My Father in heaven. Many will say to Me in that day, 'Lord, Lord, have we not prophesied in Your name, cast out demons in Your name, and done many wonders in Your name?' And then I will declare to them, 'I never knew you;

depart from Me, you who practice lawlessness!'" (Matthew 7:15-23)

It is virtually impossible to receive God's name without receiving the Word of God with boldness and sincerity. Since sound preaching is based on the Word of God, the preacher has the responsibility to preach and the congregation has the responsibility to receive the Word of God with gladness of heart. Any preaching must be in the name of the Lord. The Lord said to Moses:

> "I will raise up for them a Prophet like you from among their brethren, and will put My words in His mouth, and He shall speak to them all that I command Him. And it shall be that whoever will not hear My words, which He speaks in My name, I will require it of him. But the prophet who presumes to speak a word in My name, which I have not commanded him to speak, or who speaks in the name of other gods, that prophet shall die" (Deuteronomy 18:18-20).

Preaching false doctrine will bring dishonor to God's name because the doctrine begins with the name of the Lord.

In Jeremiah 26 the Lord commanded Jeremiah to preach to the people. The Lord instructed Jeremiah to say, "If you will not listen to Me, to walk in My law which I have set before you, to heed the words of My servants the prophets whom I sent to you....then I will make this house like Shiloh, and will make this city a curse to all the nations of the earth" (Jeremiah 26:1-6). The people became angry with Jeremiah because he was preaching the Word of God. The people then seized Jeremiah and said "you will surely die." The people said, "Why have you prophesied [preached] in the name of the Lord" (Jeremiah 26:9). Jeremiah responded by saying, "The Lord sent me here, but know for certain that if you put me to death, you will surely bring innocent blood on yourselves..." (Jeremiah 26:12). It is typical for many congregations in the modern church to take offense to the true preaching of the Word of God. Now, for the rest of the story. "So the princes and all the people said to the priests and the prophets, 'This man does not deserve to die, For he has spoken to us in the name of the Lord our God'" (Jeremiah 26:16). If God calls a man to speak truthfully, reverently, and judiciously in the name of the Lord, it is the duty of God's people to receive the Word of God with boldness and sincerity.

When a person publicly professes the Lord to be his or her God that person becomes a representative of the heavenly Father. Therefore the one who calls on the name of the Lord must be careful to protect the Father's good name with words and actions.

To violate God's law of reverence at work, in school or at home, is to reduce the worth of God's name. The reputation of God's name becomes worthless and therefore His name is used in vain.

Hypocrisy is one way to take the Lord's name in vain. Hypocrisy is pretending to call on the name of the Lord, but in reality it is just a false covering. Paul says, "They profess to know God, but in works they deny Him, being abominable, disobedient, and disqualified for every good work" (Titus 1:16). The 16th century Reformers used a Latin phrase to explain this devious practice: *simulata sanctitas duplex iniquitas*. The English translation is, "Pretended holiness is merely double wickedness."

Another way to take the Lord's name in vain is by deceitful worship. Through the mouth of Isaiah the Lord said, "Inasmuch as these people draw near with their mouths and honor Me with their lips, but have removed their hearts far from Me, and their fear toward Me is taught by the commandment of men" (Isaiah 29:13).

The name of God describes the nature and character of God. His name is necessary to develop any system of doctrine. It is necessary to make sure the system of doctrine is true to His name and based on the Word of God. Teaching a system of false doctrine concerning God, His will and His works is a violation of the third commandment. Confession of truth that is known about God is the duty of every Christian.

Complaints against God's generous providence is a complaint against the One who ordered providence. Professing Christians often complain about the events of God's providence. It rained too much or it did not rain enough. It's too hot or it's too cold and the complaints go on and on. To complain against what God provides denigrates His good name.

The misuse of God's name has a negative and positive result. Negatively, "the Lord will not hold him guiltless who takes His name in vain" (Exodus 20:7). The Old Testament penalty for this violation was death. "Whoever blasphemes the name of the Lord shall surely be put to death" (Leviticus 24:1). The judgment associated with the misuse of God's name is a fearful thought. The misuse of the name of the Lord may have eternal consequences.

The positive result of using God's name is evidence of God's saving grace. Christians will find joy in the name of the Lord our God, if His name is used in the right manner. "Let those also who love Your name be joyful in You" (Psalm 5:11).

When God grants you the ability to believe in the name of God you will have eternal life. "These things I have written to you who believe in the name of the Son of God, that you may know that you have eternal life, and that you may continue to believe in the name of the Son of God" (1 John 5:13).

Christians ought to use the name of the Lord according to the Word of God. Choose godly worship by offering true worship to the true God in His glorious name.

6. A Special Day for Worship

Remember the Sabbath day, to keep it holy. Six days you shall labor and do all your work, but the seventh day is the Sabbath of the LORD your God. In it you shall do no work: you, nor your son, nor your daughter, nor your male servant, nor your female servant, nor your cattle, nor your stranger who is within your gates. For in six days the LORD made the heavens and the earth, the sea, and all that is in them, and rested the seventh day. Therefore the LORD blessed the Sabbath day and hallowed it.
Exodus 20:8

The First commandment: worship the true and living God.

The Second commandment: worship the true and living God according to His commands.

The Third commandment: revere God's name above all other names.

If Christians seriously engage in a study of God's Word and then examine themselves very carefully, they will discover that by commission or omission, they violate those commandments. It is not really a question of reality; it is a question of degree.

There are two injunctions in the fourth commandment, "Remember the Sabbath day" and "six days you shall labor and do all your work." These two commandments are simple to understand. A careful study of the Hebrew grammatical and syntactical aspects would not change the English translation as stated above. An inquiry of the theological dimension of these two brief commandments would not reveal any secret meaning. The meaning in the Hebrew, Greek, Latin, and English bibles is plain and clear.

This particular commandment is attached with a pre-fix not found in the other commandments. God says to "remember."

God uses the word "remember" many times in the Bible. God told the Israelites to "Remember all the commandments of the Lord and do them, and that you may not follow the harlotry to which your own heart and your own eyes are inclined, and that you may remember and do all My commandments and be holy for your God" (Numbers 15:39-40). About a thousand years later the prophet Malachi said, "Remember the Law of Moses, My servant, which I commanded him in Horeb for all Israel, with the statutes and judgments" (Malachi 4:4). In each case Christians are commanded to "remember." Does it mean that God thinks they have forgotten? Probably not, because the word "remember" essentially means "to call to mind" or "be thoughtful of" in the context of Holy Scripture. For instance, how could anyone forget the law of God? It was written on the heart (Romans 2:14-15) and then it was written in stone by the finger of God (Exodus 31:18). Christians need to call God's law to mind and think about it, or to put it another way "remember."

The next important phrase is "the Sabbath day." The word "Sabbath" means to cease from or to rest. It is sometimes misinterpreted to mean that it is a day off work. The Sabbath means to change from doing one thing to doing another or to cease one thing and go to another. When the Sabbath is used in relation to God's command to keep the Sabbath, it does not mean one is to be idle or lazy on that day. It means God's people are to perform holy works for the glory of God.

The reason God's children are commanded to remember the Sabbath day is to keep it holy. The word "holy" means "to be set apart." It is derived from the Hebrew word *qadash* which is translated into English a number of different ways. The prophet Jeremiah under inspiration from God used *qadash* to "set apart" an unbelieving nation to warn Judah of His impending judgment. God sent a warning to the King of Judah to return to the Lord. God said "I will prepare destroyers against you" (Jeremiah 22:7). The words "will prepare" comes from the Hebrew word *qadash* that is translated "holy" in the fourth commandment. Literally God said to the King of Judah, "I will set apart a pagan nation to destroy

6. A Special Day for Worship

Judah if she does not repent." The Sabbath day is set apart as a special day.

Now let me re-state the fourth commandment: "Take thought of God, change what you do the other six days and keep this day set apart from the other days." The words are simple, but what do they mean in this 21st century postmodern world. They mean the same thing they did when God gave them nearly 3500 years ago.

Many liberal theologians have tried to argue that the Sabbath day was an Old Testament institution that has been abrogated. Their assertion is unaccompanied by any reasonable evidence. God established the Sabbath in the pre-fall creation. The fact that God set it apart is sufficient reason to believe the morality of the institution. The Sabbath is part of the moral law of God, because God commanded its observance prior to the Sinai law covenant recorded in Exodus chapter 20. The text from Exodus chapter 16 is worth reading for the context.

The Sabbath institution is a moral and perpetual obligation. The permanent nature of the Sabbath institution was established as a creational ordinance according to God's covenantal structure of life. God's divine plan of creation which is binding on all people of every age is three fold.

1. He established the Sabbath to insure time would be devoted to worship the Creator.
2. He established a work ethic to provide for the needs of His creatures.
3. He established marriage and family to insure the fulfillment of the great cultural mandate.

The Sabbath is the day set aside by God for His creatures, especially human creatures to worship, meditate, and call upon the name of the Lord both in the public arena and the private closet. The Lord Jesus Christ said, "The Sabbath was made for man, not man for the Sabbath" (Mark 2:27). The Sabbath principle has eternal implications.

> Then God saw everything that He had made, and indeed it was very good. So the evening and the morning were the sixth day. Thus the heavens and the earth, and all the host of them, were finished. And on the seventh day God ended His work which He had done, and He rested on the seventh day from all His work which He had done. Then God blessed the seventh day and sanctified it, because in it He rested from all His work which God had created and made. (Genesis 1:31).

Each day of creation begins and ends with these words, "So the evening and the morning were the first day." The first through the sixth day begins and ends. However there is no end to the seventh day, the Sabbath, the day the Lord rested from His creative acts.

Through the centuries the question has been raised as to whether or not God gave the Sabbath day as a ceremonial or a moral law. It was given as both. The ceremonial aspects symbolize the redemptive work of Jesus Christ. Since Christ has fulfilled all the types, figures, and symbols the ceremonial law has expired. The expiration of the ceremonial law does not mean it should be taken out of the Bible. For instance, Leviticus chapter 16 describes the Priest and his actions on the day of Atonement. The Priest wore white linen garments representing purity of the Mediator ultimately fulfilled in Jesus Christ. A sane Christian would not tear the pages of Leviticus out of the Bible because it is valuable to understand the ministry of the Lord Jesus Christ. The fourth commandment was not merely a ceremonial law. It was given to ratify the creation ordinance and clarify the duty we have to keep the Sabbath day as a special day of worship.

Francis Turretin has rightly divided the Sabbath in the Bible into three sub-divisions: The temporal, the spiritual and the eternal. The temporal refers to those Old Testament sabbatical regulations given to remind the Old Testament church of God's holiness and that God expects the proper worship at the right time. The spiritual dimension of the biblical Sabbath is peace with God and cessation of worldly employments and recreations that are perfectly legitimate at the right time. The eternal Sabbath is that in which we will be perfectly freed from our sins and the troubles of our labor in this life. The Bible says, "there remaineth a rest for the people of God" (Hebrews 4:9). True believers will eternally rest in God (*Institutes of Elenctic Theology*, by Francis Turretin, Vol. 2, p.78).

The temporal has passed and the eternal is future. The spiritual dimension of the Sabbath should be of interest to the church in general and the individual Christian in particular. Since Christians are worshipping creatures, they have three rules to follow.

1. They must have an object to worship.
2. They must know how to worship.
3. They must know when to worship.

The Lord has commanded worship to one true and living God. The Lord has given positive injunctions so they will know how to worship Him. The Lord has appointed a day for the church to worship the living God in spirit and truth according to the commandments of Scripture. The Jewish seventh day along with all other ceremonies and types were fulfilled in Christ. The great majority of the New Testament church observes on the first day of the week what the Jews celebrated on the seventh day of the week. Notice the shift in words. Celebration comes from the ceremonial laws associated with the Sabbath day. Observing the Sabbath is appropriate because of the finished work of Jesus Christ. Since there is no Bible verse to prove the shift from the seventh day to the first day of the week, Christians must depend on the deduction of principles based on the entire teaching of the Bible.

The explanation given by the 19th century theologian, Dr. R. L. Dabney is worth consideration.

> Upon the resurrection of Christ the original Sabbath obligation was by God fixed upon the first day of the week, because this day completed a second work even more

glorious and beneficent than the world's creation, by the rising of the Christ from the tomb. Hence, from that date to the end of the world the Lord's day is, by divine and apostolic authority, substantially what the Sabbath day was originally to God's people… "As it is of the law of nature, that, in general, a due proportion of time be set apart for the worship of God, so in his word, by a positive, moral and perpetual commandment, binding all men in all ages he hath particularly appointed one day in seven for a Sabbath, to be kept holy unto him: which, from the beginning of the world to the resurrection of Christ, was the last day of the week, and from the resurrection of Christ was changed into the first day of the week, which in Scripture is called the Lord's day, and is to be continued to the end of the world as the Christian Sabbath (*Discussions*, "The Christian Sabbath: Its nature, design and proper observance." by Robert Lewis Dabney, Vol. 1, p. 98-99).

Although he did not give any biblical references, he probably used the following verses to come to the conclusion.

"Now on the first day of the week, when the disciples came together to break bread, Paul, ready to depart the next day, spoke to them and continued his message until midnight" (Acts 20:7).

"On the first day of the week let each one of you lay something aside, storing up as he may prosper, that there be no collections when I come" (1 Corinthians 16:2).

"I was in the Spirit on the Lord's Day, and I heard behind me a loud voice, as of a trumpet" (Revelation 1:10).

The church has recognized the first day of the week as the Lord's Day for nearly two thousand years. Many now call it the weekend and once a year a majority of Americans will call the Lord's day, super bowl Sunday. It is a fact that many congregations

6. A Special Day for Worship

cancel or shorten worship to the true and living God to worship a football game. The Lord's Day or the Christian Sabbath is appropriate for the Christian, but nothing else is acceptable.

The Sabbath, as a theological concept, has lost its meaning over the past few generations. It is because each generation of Christian believers failed to discover the biblical meaning of this important discipline. The historical downgrade of the Sabbath obviously began in the Old Testament. God gave the moral law to Israel, the church underage, to establish the parameters of His covenant relationship. They continually violated the covenant and God eventually sent them into captivity. After seventy years of captivity, God called Nehemiah to return to Jerusalem and rebuild the city wall. After Nehemiah had labored to restore the walls so the Israelites could return and worship their God, this is what he observed.

> In those days I saw people in Judah treading wine presses on the Sabbath, and bringing in sheaves, and loading donkeys with wine, grapes, figs, and all kinds of burdens, which they brought into Jerusalem on the Sabbath day. And I warned them about the day on which they were selling provisions. Men of Tyre dwelt there also, who brought in fish and all kinds of goods, and sold them on the Sabbath to the children of Judah, and in Jerusalem. Then I contended with the nobles of Judah, and said to them, "What evil thing is this that you do, by which you profane the Sabbath day? Did not your fathers do thus, and did not our God bring all this disaster on us and on this city? Yet you bring added wrath on Israel by profaning the Sabbath." (Nehemiah 13:15-17)

The previous generations had abused the Sabbath which was one of the reasons God allowed the Babylonians to enslave the Israelites. Profaning the Sabbath was evidence of and still is evidence of rebellion against God. Nehemiah went so far as to take action against the people. Nehemiah made a risky move by threatening to shut down commerce if the people did not stop abusing the Sabbath. Nehemiah took action to keep the Sabbath from desecration and abuse for the future stability of the Sabbath to coming generations. Are we, like Nehemiah, willing to warn Christians about Sabbath day abuse?

When the Puritans came to this country they called it the Sabbath day or the Lord's day, but now days it is called Sunday. Since the founding of the United States each generation has gradually devolved upon the next generation a diminished view of the Sabbath. Blue laws were initially established to protect the Sabbath. In 1961 the Supreme Court ruled to ease restrictions of the blue laws. Within twenty years the Supreme Court ruled it legal to kill babies. Twenty years later the nation has forgotten to remember the God of creation and salvation. The Sabbath is a friend to religion; it is not the enemy. We should think of the Sabbath as the spiritual jubilee in our lives. It should remind us of heaven.

How tragic that the disease *morbus Sabbaticus* or more commonly known as "Sunday sickness" has infected a large number of professing Christians. Interestingly enough this sickness seems to never last more than 24 hours. It never interferes with appetites. It never affects the eyes - especially on Super Bowl Sunday. A doctor is never needed – It's self healing within a few hours. After a few attacks it may become chronic or even fatal.

The church will be wise to follow the advice of the Westminster assembly that issued a warning to the seventeenth century church.

> This Sabbath is then kept holy unto the Lord, when men, after a due preparing of their hearts, and ordering of their common affairs beforehand, do not only observe an holy rest all the day from their own works, words, and thoughts about their worldly employments and recreations; but also are taken up the whole time in the public and private exercises of his worship, and in the duties of necessity and mercy. (*Westminster Confession of Faith*, chapter 21, section 8)

6. A Special Day for Worship

The Bible instructs Christians both negatively and positively concerning the Sabbath. Positively, the Sabbath commandment demands hard work. "Six days you shall labor and do all your work" (Exodus 20:9). God calls His people to work hard, all six days, not five days, and then all the work will be finished. If Christians did all their work in six days there would be no need to work on the seventh. The biblical work ethic has been practically ignored by the church, because she ignores the morality of the Sabbath. It is morally binding that God commands us to rest from our work on the Sabbath, but He also commands us to work six days.

Negatively the Bible says, "In it [the Sabbath] you shall do no work" (Exodus 20:8). If Christians work needlessly on the Sabbath, they rob God of the sacred time He has given them. There are works of necessity such as caring for the sick, helping those in need, or other things that are necessary to love God and your neighbor.

The church has become lackadaisical about Sabbath abuse. Although the church is not responsible for instituting blue laws for the nation, she ought to be willing to tell her members to avoid buying, selling and working on the Lord's day, treating it no different than any other day of the week. Christians ought to remember the Sabbath after a due preparing of their hearts, and ordering of their common affairs. Christians should prepare for the Lord's day by reading and meditating on the Word of God.

On the Sabbath day protect yourself against the distraction of this world and give your attention to heavenly things. Put aside those things that distract you from receiving God's means of grace through the preaching, sacraments, and prayer.

Christianity is burdened with special days. They are all unbiblical. Scripture does not reveal, even by inference, that Christians have another day for collective worship other than the Sabbath or the first day now called Sunday.

The appointment to celebrate those special festival days as a day of worship is merely the pleasure of man-made opinion. Man-made tradition without any divine precept is often the reason for special days of worship. Once man decides to make one day special over another day, then where does it stop? What regulates special days? The great church theologian Francis Turretin sets forth an argument that deserves attention.

> It is one thing to make mention of the conception, nativity, death, resurrection and ascension of Christ on certain days in discourses to the people and this to embrace the opportunity of exhorting, consoling instructing Christians to edification, piety, patience and holiness. It is another, however, to make and by established law to impose necessarily upon Christians festivals. . .to constitute these a part of divine worship as more holy than other days" (*Institutes of Elenctic Theology,* by Francis Turretin, Vol. 2, p. 107).

Let Christ be the joy of your Sabbath, then you will have no other reason to celebrate other days. There is no joy in the Sabbath without Christ. There appears to be many professing Christians that do not exhibit joy on the Sabbath. Maybe they are without Christ! Make the Sabbath your delight in Christ. Let the redemptive work of Christ be the joy of your Sabbath. Keeping the Sabbath will reflect your love for the Savior.

7. The Law of Authority

Honor your father and your mother, that your days may be long upon the land which the Lord your God is giving you.

Exodus 20:12

    The first four commandments are given to teach Christians to worship God according to His standards. The next six commandments regulate and explain human relationships. The fifth commandment is like a bridge between the first four commandments and the last five commandments. All ten of them will serve the child of God to make godly choices.

    A few years ago the Ten Commandments made news headlines in Alabama when Judge Roy Moore refused to remove a wall plaque of the Ten Commandments from his courtroom. Why are people so divided over the public display of the Ten Commandments? We would probably find the answer if we ask another question? Do people understand the Ten Commandments? More specifically, do *Christians* understand the Ten Commandments?

    If the unbeliever does not believe the Ten Commandments, then he or she ought not to complain if somebody steals all their money; So much for the notion that the Ten Commandments are invalid. The reason most people are not outright thieves is because of natural law. (See Romans 2:14-15 discussed in detail in chapter sixteen.)

    Survey after survey indicates that Christians believe they live by the Ten Commandments, but the majority of those surveyed could not name the Ten Commandments. Maybe they simply do not understand the doctrine and application of the doctrine. Maybe they are simply not telling the truth. In two national surveys conducted by Barna Research, one among adults and one among teenagers, people were asked if they believe that there are moral absolutes that are unchanging or that moral truth is relative to the circumstances. By a 3-to-1 margin (64% vs. 22%) adults said truth is always relative to the person and their situation. The perspective was even more lopsided among teenagers, 83% of whom said moral truth depends on the circumstances, and only 6% of whom said moral truth is absolute.

If you take the "truth is relative" theory to its logical end, words can mean anything you want them to mean. For instance, the fifth commandment does not say obey your parents, even though it is sometimes expressed in those terms. It says, "honor your father and mother."

Father is a title given by God and it is distinct from mother. The fifth commandment is a general principle expressed by familial language. The language of the family is commonly used in the Bible to show the relationship to spiritual things. There are references to "the whole family in heaven and earth" (Ephesians 3:15). Jesus said, "Whoever does the will of My Father in heaven is My brother and sister and mother" (Matthew 12:50). God's children have a spiritual family as well as an earthly family.

The egalitarian culture in our nation has practically reduced the biblical concept of family into a waste land of individualism. The word egalitarian refers to "equality of all people." The word "equality" was used in the French Revolution because the poor working class and wage earners were disgusted with the inequitable treatment of the poor relative to the rich. The desire to have an egalitarian society is contrary to God's Word. God created a man and a woman. In God's providence some are rich and some are poor. Different people have different gifts. God never intended for everybody to be equal. The only egalitarian thread that every person shares is they are born into this life as sinners in the sight of God and in need of His saving grace. The main point of understanding egalitarianism is that it despises and rejects the authority of God.

God did not just create a person; He created a family that began with a father and mother. Children followed as the result of this unique union. The children are then under the authority of the father and mother. The fifth commandment, like the other nine must be interpreted in the context of the whole Bible. If Christians consult the whole counsel of God, they will find this commandment is a theological concept that may be best summarized as the law of authority. The biblical doctrine of authority is a general principle. The fifth commandment teaches that authority demands respect.

Obviously a person cannot worship without submission to authority. There are two parties involved in worship. There must be a submissive subject and there must be an honorable object. In Christian worship the honorable object is God. It is God who has ultimate authority. One verse summarizes this magnificent truth. In the book of Ephesians Paul explains how God exalted the second person of the trinity, Jesus Christ to be "far above all principality and power and might and dominion… not only in this age but the age to come" (Ephesians 1:21).

The general principle of this commandment begins with God's authority over all of creation, including all men and angels. When an Army officer wanted Jesus to heal his servant he told Jesus to say the word and the servant would be healed. The officer understood that Jesus had the authority to heal and stated it by analogy. He told Jesus, "For I also am a man under authority, having soldiers under me. And I say to this one, 'Go' and He goes; and to another 'come' and he comes; and to my servant 'Do this' and he does it." Just as the officer had authority over certain people, he knew that Jesus had the ultimate authority over life (Luke 7:1-10).

The fifth commandment mandates the respect and honor due to those who have authority. An understanding of the biblical doctrine of authority, especially in the context of this commandment is necessary for order in society. Human nature is such that pride will protest against authority. Furthermore, this commandment is a necessary condition if Christians expect to understand the next five commandments on human relationships. Murder, adultery, robbery, dishonesty and jealousy will certainly prevail unless respect, honor, and authority are the controlling factors in our relationships with other people. The word "honor" deserves special attention. The word "honor" comes from a

Hebrew word which is often translated "glorify" in the Old Testament. The root word demonstrates "heaviness" or "weightiness" of character. It describes the profound loftiness of the honorable object. Given the grammar associated with the word honor in the context with which it is used, it means nothing less than reverence of the highest degree when it pertains to God and respect to the highest degree when it refers to God's people.

The fifth commandment is foundational to all the other commandments, because it is not possible to worship God and having meaningful human relationships unless there is subjection to authority. If Christians reject the concept of authority, they cannot hope to honor anything or anybody.

The word "honor" in Exodus 20:12 is a verb, not a noun. The word "honor" requires an action by God's children. What action must they take? They are required to give respect to their father and mother which leads to obedience. The father and mother are to be honored in the same way, but not the same degree, in which they fear and reverence the Lord God almighty.

The words "father" and "mother" used in the commandment extends to represent anyone that God has placed in a position of authority. Our biological father and mother are the authors of our bodily life and so many years the preserver and protector of bodily life. The father and mother represent the principle of authority over the child from birth. Generally speaking natural parents are to be respected and obeyed for the well being of the child. There is practical utility attached to the morality of this commandment. There may be occasions that instant and exact obedience is necessary for survival.

Example: The father tells the child to stop walking for a poisonous snake is in the pathway. Instant and exact obedience will save the child. Disobedience may cause harm or possibly death.

Example: The mother tells the child to not run into the street to get the ball because heavy traffic is approaching. The survival of the child depends on obedience.

7. The Law of Authority

Children must honor and respect their natural fathers and mothers as they are the instruments of the childs well being until maturity. Order, harmony, and peace cannot exist unless we honor and obey those who possess authority, beginning with our natural father and mother. However, if earthly fathers and mothers do not honor and reverence the heavenly father, the children live in confusion.

When the time comes for the child to leave his or her father and mother and cleave to a husband or wife, then God provides others to act in the place of the father and mother. If children rebel against father and mother, they are likely to rebel against other authorities.

God has also given His children spiritual fathers with authority to maintain peace and carry out the purpose, mission, and ministry of the church. The spiritual fathers of the church are the pastors and elders. The Lord gives the spiritual care of His children to pastors and elders. The Word of God instructs elders to, "take heed to yourselves and to all the flock, among which the Holy Spirit has made you overseers, to shepherd the church of God which He purchased with His own blood" (Acts 20:28). When Elijah was being taken up by a whirlwind into heaven, Elisha said "My father, my father, the chariot of Israel and its horsemen" (2 Kings 2:12). Elijah was Elisha's spiritual father. He showed Elisha the way of salvation through the Word of God. When Paul the Apostle wrote to Philemon, the apostle referred to Onesimus as his spiritual son (Philemon 10). The office of spiritual fathers is worthy of due honor. Honor them for their work. The Apostle Paul tells the church to "recognize those who labor among you, and are over you in the Lord and admonish you, and to esteem them very highly in love for their work's sake" (1 Thessalonians. 5:13). Honor them by conforming to the doctrine they teach, if the teaching is biblical.

Christians must honor not only their natural fathers and mothers, and their spiritual fathers, but they must also honor civil and political fathers. God in His wisdom and by His grace has placed earthly governors over His people to preserve civil and political harmony in all earthly kingdoms.

Christians should be humble and modest, but often they elevate themselves with pride and arrogance. They are not willing to subjugate themselves. They lack self discipline. For that reason God commands his people to honor, respect, and obey rulers.

Disorder, chaos and confusion are common among the nations of the world. It was that way when there was no king in Israel and "every man did that which was right in his own eyes" (Judges 17:6). Ungodly ambition and individualism are enemies of order and harmony. The purpose of the law of authority is to maintain mutual order and respect for those of authority and those who are subordinate to that authority.

The New Testament gives some clarification and commentary to the Old Testament moral law.

> Children, obey your parents in the Lord, for this is right. Honor your father and mother," which is the first commandment with promise: "that it may be well with you and you may live long on the earth." And you, fathers, do not provoke your children to wrath, but bring them up in the training and admonition of the Lord. Bondservants, be obedient to those who are your masters according to the flesh, with fear and trembling, in sincerity of heart, as to Christ; not with eye service, as men-pleasers, but as bondservants of Christ, doing the will of God from the heart, with goodwill doing service, as to the Lord, and not to men, knowing that whatever good anyone does, he will receive the same from the Lord, whether he is a slave or free. And you, masters, do the same things to them, giving up threatening, knowing that your own Master also is in heaven, and there is no partiality with Him. (Ephesians 6:1-9)

The New Testament resounds the Old Testament doctrine of honor and respect to those in authority. The New Testament brings obedience to the front of the discussion. The New Testament explains the "land" in terms of the new covenant. Moses, speaking in the shadows of the Old Covenant referred to the "land

7. The Law of Authority

which the Lord Your God is giving you" (Exodus 20:12). In the light of the New Covenant the "land" changes to the "earth" (Ephesians 6:3). The New Testament explicitly gives an explanation of how the law of authority applies to various aspects of life. Paul specifically explains the servant/master relationship. (See Ephesians 6:5-9).

The parent, the schoolmaster, the teacher, the pastor, the elder and the government official are examples of those who hold offices of authority. God commands his children to honor and respect biological fathers and mothers; likewise to spiritual fathers, civil fathers and political fathers. God also demands those in authority to discharge their duties to be esteemed worthy of honor.

Jesus did not always honor the men who called themselves religious leaders or spiritual fathers. In fact, Jesus demonstrated his disdain towards them with contempt and disrespect. "Woe to you, scribes and Pharisees, hypocrites!..." (See Matthew 23:13-36). Over and over again Jesus exposes their hypocrisy. Jesus even calls them serpents and a brood of vipers. To call someone a poisonous snake was as vile and unlikeable as possible without sin. Jesus then suggested that they would be condemned to hell. These were religious leaders holding an office of authority. Blind obedience will end in tyranny and suffering. Authority will always accompany the power to rule. At the beginning of the discourse in which Jesus condemned the religious leaders (Matthew 23:1ff) Jesus also said, "The scribes and the Pharisees sit in Moses' seat. Therefore whatever they tell you to observe, that observe and do, but do not do according to their works" (Matthew 23:2-3). It is the regulative principle, the Word of God that determines due obedience. It is from the Word of God that the church should constitute the law of authority.

Christians must be certain, very certain, that they believe and act in accordance to God's law, because God's law is the final authority. They must obey that authority, because all other authority is based on God's law. If your father or mother instructs you to disobey God's law, you must disobey your father or mother. If your employer tells you to lie or cheat in order to make a profit, you must disobey your employer. If the government commands you to abort your babies, you must disobey the government. If men set up their own rules, regulations, and authority that are contrary to the Word of God, those rules and regulations will bring havoc and suffering to the church and to society.

The law of authority is perhaps the most complicated of all the commandments because it requires submission to authority. The pride of the sinful human nature resists authority. Therefore, "Humble yourselves in the sight of the Lord, and He will lift you up" (James 4:8).

Consider everything the Bible has to say about this injunction for understanding the full counsel of God is the key to understanding the law of authority. If Christians submit to God's authority, it is pleasing to God and He promises an inheritance in the kingdom of God.

The law of authority has a promise suffixed to it. The promise to the Old Testament congregation was "that your days may be long upon the land which the Lord your God is giving you" (Exodus 20:12). The promise to the New Testament congregation was "that is may be well with you and you may live long on the earth" (Ephesians 6:3). Everyone that has ever read these two verses side by side probably wondered why the Old Testament refers to the land of Canaan and the New Testament refers to the whole earth. The answer is very simple. One was for the people of the God under the old covenant known as Israel and the other was for the people of God under the new covenant known as the church. Under God's covenant plan, all His children belong to him regardless of where they sojourn.

The promise attached to this commandment also brings out another covenantal concept that is also very easy to understand: right relationships are necessary for peace. Right relationships are necessary for peace regardless of the location of the property. When the covenant is fully consummated there will be peace in a place called "the new heavens and the new earth" (2 Peter 3:13). Human relationships depend on fundamentals like respecting order and respecting authority.

Christians ought to pray and ask the Lord to have mercy on them and incline their hearts to honor the law of authority. For if they expect and desire to be God's people, they must expect and desire to be governed by Jesus Christ. The Lord Jesus Christ redeemed His church. He procured salvation for God's people so they might love His authority.

8. The Value of Life

You shall not murder

Exodus 20:13

The first four commandments describe the unique and ultimate relationship with God. God gave His people the Ten Commandments because they are special to Him. God commands His people to know Him and to worship Him according to His instructions. He instructs His people to honor, cherish and love Him. God gave His special people a special day to worship. God gave His special people the first four commandments so they would know how to live *Coram Deo*, "before the face of God." The Lord Jesus Christ referred to these four commandments as the "first and great commandment." "You shall love the LORD your God with all your heart, and all your soul, and with all your mind" (Matthew 22:37-38).

The fifth commandment is the law of authority. It gives God's people the general principle from which harmony and order is established so that God will be glorified. The fifth commandment explains how God has ultimate authority in life, but it also introduces how God's people relate to and interact with one another.

The sixth through the tenth commandment sets the standard for godly attitudes and behavior for God's people. "You shall not murder" is the standard for Christians to understand and protect the value of life. Life is valuable, because it is a gift from God. Human life has innate qualities that everyone, especially Christians, should recognize and respect. The greatest gifts that God gave the human race are rational and moral abilities. The sin of the human race turned the rational into irrational and the moral into the immoral. The greatest gift God gives His special people is His redeeming grace through the Lord Jesus Christ. Under the old covenant they were Israel and in the new covenant they are the church. The old and the new must understand the rule to preserve life. If Christians follow the rule of life, the value of life will increase.

Michael Horton used this example to explain one of the major differences between Judaism and Christianity. The Rabbi said, "we Jews believe you have to actually commit the physical act by violating the Ten Commandments. You Christians believe that you've committed a sin just by desiring or thinking about it. If that is the case we'd be sinning all the time." Horton replied, "Precisely, we are sinning all the time. That's the whole point."

George Barna conducted a survey of 1013 professing adult Christians. 93% said they did not commit murder. Maybe 942 were Jews, which would be 93% of the 1013 so called professing Christians. Either that or those Christians answering the poll have not studied the Bible thoroughly and systematically enough to understand the commandment. Is it possible that they have never received proper biblical teaching on the subject?

There are several Hebrew words used in the Old Testament to describe the act of taking the life of another person. The words murder, kill, slay, and destroy may describe the physical act of taking someone's life, but it is also used as a figure of speech. The Psalmist said, "Yet for Your sake we are killed all day long" (Psalm 44:22). The word "kill" was used as a metaphor to describe the suffering for the sake of a righteous God.

The physical act of murder, killing, slaying or destroying someone's life may come from a source that is not immoral. For instance, God's judgment on the Egyptians was the death of "all the firstborn in the land of Egypt" (Exodus 13:15). There are many other illustrations. If one person is killed in an auto accident because the other person had a sudden heart attack, the murder is not from an immoral source. If someone is killed by a tornado, the murder is not immoral. The heart attack and the tornado occurred because of a depraved creation; however, the event was not an immoral motivation by a rational creature.

The commandment that prohibits one sinner from killing another sinner is most necessary to preserve life. This

8. The Value of Life

commandment does not define or explain the doctrine of just war. From the doctrine of this commandment, one may derive from the full counsel of God a better understanding of the value of life according to God's infinite perfection. The discipline of using the proper tools to interpret Scripture and the gift of discernment is necessary to grasp the teaching of this subject. God told Adam and Eve not to eat or touch the tree in the midst of the garden. If they did touch or eat it they would die. It is no doubt that this referred to the physical death of the body. However, it also referred to the spiritual death of a favorable relationship with the Creator. Paul refers to this spiritual death in his letter to the Romans (See Romans 5:12ff).

The concept of murder may be traced to the entrance of sin into the world. Jesus said Satan was a murderer from the beginning (John 8:44). Satan attempts to deceive people so as to destroy the soul, not the body. We travel on dangerous ground when we ignore simple principles in biblical interpretation. It appears that most Christians believe this commandment is primarily concerned with physical death. The Lord Jesus Christ said, "Do not fear those who kill the body but cannot kill the soul. But rather fear Him who is able to destroy both soul and body in Hell" (Matthew 10:28). The Bible teaches that God is concerned for proximate matters in this secular life; however He is much more interested in the ultimate matters pertaining to eternal life. God understands the value of life. Do you?

There are two dimensions to the commandment, "you shall not murder." The first dimension is physical and the second dimension is spiritual. In the first dimension God's children are commanded not to inflict hurt or injury to their own bodies, nor the bodies of other people. Obviously, this commandment calls attention to the body and the important function of the body in this present world. God has chosen to use human beings to accomplish some of His ordained mission and ministry on earth. Their bodies have to be preserved to be useful. It pleases God to use people, to carry out the purpose, mission, and ministry of the church. Furthermore, the body is the temple of the Holy Spirit so we must treat the body with respect and prudence. God created the human body so that God's image may be expressed in terms of existence, self consciousness, knowledge, the power to make choices, and all the actions that proceed from knowledge and choices. The body is valuable in every respect.

The second dimension commands God's people not to murder the character, name or reputation of another person. Jesus gives a full explanation of this very dangerous crime.

> You have heard that it was said to those of old, 'You shall not murder, and whoever murders will be in danger of the judgment.' But I say to you that whoever is angry with his brother without a cause shall be in danger of the judgment. And whoever says to his brother, 'Raca!' shall be in danger of the council. But whoever says, 'You fool!' shall be in danger of hell fire. Therefore if you bring your gift to the altar, and there remember that your brother has something against you, leave your gift there before the altar, and go your way. First be reconciled to your brother, and then come and offer your gift. Agree with your adversary quickly, while you are on the way with him, lest your adversary deliver you to the judge, the judge hand you over to the officer, and you be thrown into prison. Assuredly, I say to you, you will by no means get out of there till you have paid the last penny. (Matthew 5:21-26)

Jesus used figures of speech in this discourse so the application would not be limited to particular circumstances. He speaks to a general audience about the religious leaders of His day. "You have heard that is was said" is a reference to the teaching of those same religious leaders. It is clear from the words of Jesus that the heart sin of murder is just as evil as the hand sin of murder.

It is a cruel and vicious thing to murder a man in his name. Gossip, slander, and back-biting are commonly practiced by professing Christians. The sinful fallen nature seems to delight in the failure and misfortune of others. The Bible has a warning not to

8. The Value of Life

take delight in the misfortune of other people. Job issues a warning in negative terms.

> If I have kept the poor from their desire, or caused the eyes of the widow to fail, or eaten my morsel by myself, so that the fatherless could not eat of it; if I have seen anyone perish for lack of clothing, or any poor man without covering, if I have raised my hand against the fatherless, when I say I had help in the gate; Then let my arm fall from my shoulder, let my arm be torn from the socket, for destruction from God is a terror to me. (Job 31:16-23)

Then King Lemuel's Mother states the duty in positive terms: "Open your mouth for the speechless, and plead the cause of the poor and needy" (Proverbs 31:8-9).

When we talk about someone's private affairs and especially a default or failure of some kind, we are guilty of the sin of gossip. It is a violation of the sixth commandment. Then there are those Christians who slander other people. When you make a malicious false characterization of someone else, it is slander. It is a violation of the sixth commandment. Back-biting is to attack another person's reputation or character in his or her absence. It is a violation of sixth commandment. Rather than murder, consider life; consider the value of life. Make a godly choice and follow the teaching found in the Word of God. The Bible says, "if a man is overtaken in any trespass, you who are spiritual restore such a one in a spirit of gentleness, considering yourself, lest you also be tempted. Bear one another's burdens and so fulfill the law of Christ" (Galatians 6:1-2).

The sins that lead to murder are the ones that come from ignorance of the law or an inadequate understanding of God's Word. Furthermore, they are distinguished as heart sins. Three of the most dangerous sins that lead to murder are anger, envy, and hatred.

Anger is an emotional response that may have merit or it may cause sinful behavior. It is the selfish greedy ego that provokes anger. When Jacob delivered his final prophecy to his children, he said some of them were cruel and conniving. "For in their anger they slew a man...Cursed be their anger, for it is fierce; and their wrath, for it is cruel" (Genesis 49:5-6). It is not a question of whether or not the murder of Hamor and Shechem was just; it was a question of the attitude and motive of the heart. Unadvised and uncontrolled anger will seldom lead to the murder of the body, but will very often lead to the murder of someone's character. Jesus left His church with a very solemn warning. "But I say to you that whoever is angry with his brother without cause shall be in danger of the judgment" (Matthew 5:22).

Envy is another sin that causes people to murder. It was envious Cain who murdered his brother (Genesis 4:4-8). "Wrath is cruel and anger a torrent, but who is able to stand before jealousy?" (Proverbs 27:4).

Hatred is another reason people murder other people. Remember the story of Haman and Mordecai. Haman hated Mordecai because he would not bow to Haman. Do you remember the rest of the story? Haman sought to kill innocent people because Haman hated Mordecai (See Esther 3:1-15). Hatred has ruined many a good name in the church. "Whoever hates his brother is a murderer, and you know that no murderer has eternal life abiding in him" (1 John 3:15).

Certainly there are other things that lead to physical murder and character assassination, but anger, envy, and hatred stand in front of all others. These sins are forbidden by the sixth commandment.

There are many ways to murder another person. You may murder by your own physical strength. You may use your mind to plot another person's death; either the death of the body or death of character and name. "Woe to those who scheme iniquity, who work out evil on their beds! When morning comes they do it, for it is in the power of their hands" (Micah 2:1). Murder by use of the tongue is popular in the contemporary church. The tongue "is an unruly evil, full of deadly poison" (James 3:8). Murder with the pen has not been very popular, but with the onslaught of instant communication, the pen, email, texting, will likely take the place of the tongue. King David had Uriah murdered by writing a letter to Joab so that during battle Joab was to "set Uriah in the forefront of the hottest battle and retreat from him, that he may be struck down and die" (2 Samuel 11:14-17). Another way to murder is by agreeing with the actual hit man. It occurs if someone consents to the murder. If you stand by and allow someone to murder another person's character, you are part of the plot.

It is so easy to murder the good name and character of someone by standing by and not defending the truth. Cruel mean-spirited remarks that have no basis is murder without a cause. It is a crime and it brings disgrace to the individual and the church. This does not mean Christians should avoid the truth. It does mean Christians should use biblical processes to settle disputes without resorting to hidden murder such as gossip, slander, and back-biting.

The best way to overcome the temptation to murder is by following the instructions in the Bible. Rather than criticize, find fault, and talk about the sin of the other person, why not follow the biblical instructions and bear the burden of sin for one who has fallen in sin. The best way to prevent murder is to obey God and turn your back to Satan's lies.

Obviously, this commandment is not just an ethical code. It is concerned with how Christians relate to other people and especially God's people. Many evangelical Christians consider themselves pro life. But, are they pro life? They get upset when they hear about the mass murder of unborn children, especially those taken in the last stages of the pregnancy. The question lingers on; do they really value life, at any stage from the cradle to the grave? Do they march for the unborn in the morning and murder the brethren in the afternoon?

Some Christians are concerned about the increase of murder by the hands of young teenagers. Yet, Christians kill one another by thought, word, gesture and speech without the blink of an eye.

Christian A must be very careful to claim to be a pro life conservative when he or she allows Christian B to be murdered in their own church. If you really want to be pro life then love your neighbor as yourself and protect him or her from injury and hurt of any kind. Christians should value life because Christ was willing to die that they may have life. Without Christ we shall surely die. With Christ we shall surely live.

9. The Value of Right Relationships

You shall not commit adultery.

Exodus 20:14

Human life celebrates consciousness with intercourse. Before you take a deep plunge into the world of confusion, just take a deep breath and think, think, and think some more. You may have misinterpreted the word intercourse.

Webster's definition for intercourse is, "dealings or communication between individuals, groups, countries, etc." It also means an interchange of thoughts, feelings, etc... Finally, Webster says it may refer to "sexual relations." Which one or combination of them did I have in mind when I said, "human life celebrates consciousness with intercourse." Words must be interpreted within their context, not what our minds conjure up out of context. A baby comes into this world normally conscious of the world around him or her. The baby immediately develops relationships with mother and father. The baby will spend the rest of his or her life in a relationship with God and with other human beings. The relationship will be godly or ungodly. The great need for every person is to learn and use the rules of relationship that conduce meaningful intercourse in life. It is the great need for every Christian to learn the value of reliable relationships.

The Bible describes the value of a reliable relationship before sin entered into the world. This is how it worked in paradise. "Therefore a man shall leave his father and mother and be joined to his wife, and they shall become one flesh" (Genesis 2:24). Dr. Buck Hatch, a long time Bible teacher at Columbia International University, described the marriage relationship in terms of leave, cleave and become one. The man must "leave" his father and mother; it establishes the importance of the marriage relationship. The man must "cleave" to his wife; it reveals the permanent nature of the marriage relationship. The two shall "become one" shows the intimate nature of the marriage relationship. It was a picture of two people who understood the value of reliable relationships.

Sin entered into the world and the reliable relationship turned into a ruined relationship. Before the fall into sin two people had a beautiful, marvelous, and pure relationship with God and with each other. After the fall into sin the same two people hid from God and they hid from each other. They began to blame each other for the failed relationship (Genesis 3:8-24). It was just a few generations until man was committing adultery.

Global instant communication technology seems determined to bring bad news as often as possible. Sexual promiscuity makes the headlines on a regular basis. Many believe that promiscuous activity is greater now than ever before. Read the Bible and you will learn that a sexually promiscuous society is not anything new. There is strong biblical evidence that the Lord destroyed Sodom because of sexual perversion.

The seventh commandment is one of the most abused of all the commandments. That does not mean it is violated any more than the others. Many contemporary Christians, especially some of the most pious acting preachers treat it as if it was the unforgiveable sin. The previous sentence is a statement of hyperbole, an exaggerated statement to make a point. It is true that many Christians act as if the seventh commandment is worse in the eyes of God than violating any of the other commandments.

This commandment will be examined in light of the sin that provokes adultery. That sin is unfaithfulness. It is necessary to consider the unfaithfulness of a man or woman to each other and unfaithfulness to God. The unfaithfulness of men and women in relation to each other is called physical adultery. Unfaithfulness to God is called spiritual adultery.

The Hebrew word *naaph*, used in the Old Testament, may refer to the physical act of an extra-marital sexual relationship. The word is rarely used to describe a specific event. The Bible uses terminology like "Reuben went and lay with Bilhah" (Genesis 35:22). The Hebrew word *naaph* is used occasionally in the Old Testament as a figure of speech. The Greek word *moicheuo* and its

9. The Value of Right Relationships 73

other word forms primarily refer to adultery, but also refers to the spiritual life of the church (See Mark 8:38). The seventh commandment has physical and spiritual application.

The Bible reveals several examples of men, and primarily men, who could not control their sexual lust. Jacob was critical of his son Rueben who had sex with Jacob's concubine (Genesis 35:22). A concubine was a live-in mistress. Jacob's marriage to Leah and Rachel and having sexual relationships with a live-in mistress is contrary to the leave, cleave, and become one manifesto found in the early chapters of Genesis (Genesis 2:24). Jacob failed to set a godly example. Samson's marriage to a Philistine woman shows his unfaithfulness to the covenant of law (Deuteronomy 7:3). Then there was his sin with Delilah (Judges 16). David committed adultery with Bathsheba, had her husband killed, and lied about it. These three men represent men universally. However, they stand out as men having favor with God. They obviously asked forgiveness and God was gracious to them (Malachi 1:2; Hebrews 11:32; 2 Samuel 12:13-14).

The sin of adultery infects societies to various degrees. The cause and effect relationship is a factor. As instruments of sexual deviancy become more popular, then they become more popular and more popular, and etc. Once the society of people ignores the standard for behavior, the easier it is to deviate and it simply becomes easier; then the exponential factor comes into play.

Sexual instruction in Scripture belongs to the father and mother. They alone have the responsibility to teach their children the role of the male and female within the covenant family structure and the moral misuse or abuse of sex.

The location of the seventh commandment among the Ten Commandments may be worth a brief word. It is between the sixth commandment on life and the eighth commandment on property. The sixth commandment is a precept about the value of life. The biblical doctrine instructs God's people about their own and their neighbor's lives and how the two relate to each other. The eighth commandment is a precept about the value of a sacred trust. The doctrine instructs God's people about their own and their neighbor's property and how the two relate to each other. The seventh commandment is a precept about the virtue of our own and our neighbor's bodies and how the two relate to each other. The body is the temple of the Holy Spirit therefore it is of great value. The moral duty contained in the seventh commandment requires God's children to guard and protect their body against abuses as well as the body of their neighbor.

The majority of cases of adultery and all illegitimate sexual practices take time to plan and execute, therefore it is a planned and deliberate act. Adultery is a needless act. Paul explained this principle to the Corinthian Church. "Nevertheless, because of sexual immorality, let each man have his own wife, and let each woman have her own husband" (1 Corinthians 7:2). Why be guilty of sexual sins when there is no reason to be. It is inexcusable. It is like a rich man stealing money when there is no need.

Christians may elevate the sin of adultery to the highest of all sins. It is a sign of spiritual immaturity and biblical ignorance to think in those terms. Moses, the prophets, the apostles and especially the Lord Jesus Christ taught plainly that sin encompasses many evils. One of His clearest statements is in the gospel of Matthew. "For out of the heart proceed evil thoughts, murders, adulteries, fornications, thefts, false witness, and blasphemies. These are the things which defile a man…" (Matthew 15:19). There is no priority for the evil of the various sins. They are all evil in the sight of God. Each of the sins that Jesus mentioned will have an effect on ones relationship with God and with other people. Adultery like any other sin will have its effect. I will mention just a few of the effects that adultery provokes.

> It causes people to steal from their neighbor.
> It causes moral corruption.
> It makes the human resemble an animal.
> It may cause the murder of another person.
> It causes one to squander financial resources.
> It almost always destroys a person's reputation.

9. The Value of Right Relationships

Is there any hope for those who violate the seventh commandment? The redemptive work of Jesus Christ applied to the heart of the sinner by the power of the Holy Spirit is the only way to turn an unfaithful relationship into a reliable relationship. Repent and return to the Lord; He will certainly show His great mercy, grace, and boundless love with pardon and forgiveness. The immoral woman who wiped Jesus' feet with her tears and hair found forgiveness. Jesus said, "Her sins, which are many, have been forgiven, for she loved much" (Luke 7:38ff).

Now I turn to the silent sin in the church. It is not well known or discussed, but it is spiritual adultery. What does God say about spiritual adultery? He has plenty to say. In fact, God speaks more often against spiritual adultery than He does about physical adultery. Furthermore, the evidence from Scripture indicates the consequences for spiritual adultery are more serious. The question that Christians ought to ask is: "Why is there so much silence in the church when it comes to the subject of spiritual adultery?" Why is the punishment quick and often severe for physical adultery, but no punishment for spiritual adultery? The evangelical church apparently has more concern for the temporal and physical among the brethren than they have about the permanent spiritual relationship they have with their Creator.

The words "spiritual adultery" are not found in the Bible. Neither is the word "trinity" found in the Bible, but virtually all Christians believe the doctrine of the trinity because the doctrine is derived from the full counsel of God. The study of adultery as a biblical concept begins by understanding that it involves unfaithfulness. In the marriage relationship the husband and wife are either faithful, which means no adultery, or they are unfaithful which means adultery. In the relationship of God to His child, now called a Christian, God is always faithful and incapable of being unfaithful. However, the Christian will be either faithful or unfaithful. Faithful means no spiritual adultery; unfaithful means spiritual adultery. The way to avoid spiritual adultery is to obey the first commandment: "You shall have no other gods before the true and living God."

Spiritual adultery has a long history beginning with a couple named Adam and Eve. They wanted some zip and pizzazz in religious life. They were not content with their reliable relationship with God. They had to chase after something else. Spiritual adultery is chasing after the most popular religious guru, even if he or she is an obvious fake. Spiritual adultery is chasing after the latest religious craze on the market. Spiritual adultery is believing and embracing false doctrine rather than true biblical doctrine.

Spiritual adultery has exponentially increased over the past seventy-five years. With the advancement of communication technology came the religious icons on radio and television. Now there are numerous false teachers on the internet and in the future they will be in your i-pocket device. Very few of them teach the full counsel of God. Many of them have the gift of charm. The discerning mind should remember the gift of the Devil was charm. The best way to avoid spiritual adultery is to act like a Berean. Search the Scriptures, all of them, all the time to know the truth. Then avoid a shepherd that does not know your name. The shepherd must know the sheep and have considerable personal knowledge of them.

The religious marketplace has a large variety of religious views; you may choose any of them. There is Hinduism, Buddhism, Islam, and dozens of other world religions that offer their particular take on the value of life and reliable relationships. Then, of course, there is Christianity. It has a smorgasbord of religious views to choose from. There is wide variety: Roman Catholic, Anglican, Jehovah's Witness, Latter Day Saints, Pentecostal, Evangelical and hundreds of others. Among evangelicals there is a wide choice of religious views, too many to list in this brief work. Spiritual adultery is chasing after the religious view that pleases "you" the most; the one that appeals to "you". Avoid this type of spiritual adultery by choosing the one that consistently, and the operative word is consistently, teaches from the whole counsel of God. Make a godly choice and choose the religious view that pleases God.

The worst form of spiritual adultery is found on the inside. It happens when the sinful heart is disinclined from the Word of

9. The Value of Right Relationships

God. For a remedy pray as the Psalmist prayed, "Give me understanding and I shall keep Your law…Incline my heart to Your testimonies…" (Psalm 119:34-36). Christians are commanded not to be "tossed to and fro and carried about with every wind of doctrine, by the trickery of men" (Ephesians 4:14).

The Bible has numerous references to adulterous Israel in the Old Testament and the adulterous church in the New Testament. The Old Testament prophets provide a graphic description of Israel's unfaithfulness and the consequences of her spiritual adultery. The Parable in Ezekiel chapter sixteen summarizes the relationship of Israel to God.

> Then the word of the LORD came to me, saying, "Son of man, make known to Jerusalem her abominations and say, 'Thus says the Lord GOD to Jerusalem, "Your origin and your birth are from the land of the Canaanite, your father was an Amorite and your mother a Hittite. As for your birth, on the day you were born your navel cord was not cut, nor were you washed with water for cleansing; you were not rubbed with salt or even wrapped in cloths. No eye looked with pity on you to do any of these things for you, to have compassion on you. Rather you were thrown out into the open field, for you were abhorred on the day you were born. When I passed by you and saw you squirming in your blood, I said to you while you were in your blood, 'Live!' Yes, I said to you while you were in your blood, 'Live!' I made you numerous like plants of the field. Then you grew up, became tall and reached the age for fine ornaments; your breasts were formed and your hair had grown. Yet you were naked and bare. Then I passed by you and saw you, and behold, you were at the time for love; so I spread My skirt over you and covered your nakedness. I also swore to you and entered into a covenant with you so that you became Mine," declares the Lord GOD. "Then I bathed you with water, washed off your blood from you and anointed you with oil. I also clothed you with embroi-

dered cloth and put sandals of porpoise skin on your feet; and I wrapped you with fine linen and covered you with silk. I adorned you with ornaments, put bracelets on your hands and a necklace around your neck. I also put a ring in your nostril, earrings in your ears and a beautiful crown on your head. Thus you were adorned with gold and silver, and your dress was of fine linen, silk and embroidered cloth. You ate fine flour, honey and oil; so you were exceedingly beautiful and advanced to royalty. Then your fame went forth among the nations on account of your beauty, for it was perfect because of My splendor which I bestowed on you," declares the Lord GOD. But you trusted in your beauty and played the harlot because of your fame, and you poured out your harlotries on every passer-by who might be willing. You took some of your clothes, made for yourself high places of various colors and played the harlot on them, which should never come about nor happen. You also took your beautiful jewels made of My gold and of My silver, which I had given you, and made for yourself male images that you might play the harlot with them. Then you took your embroidered cloth and covered them, and offered My oil and My incense before them. Also My bread which I gave you, fine flour, oil and honey with which I fed you, you would offer before them for a soothing aroma; so it happened," declares the Lord GOD. "Moreover, you took your sons and daughters whom you had borne to Me and sacrificed them to idols to be devoured. Were your harlotries so small a matter? You slaughtered My children and offered them up to idols by causing them to pass through the fire. Besides all your abominations and harlotries you did not remember the days of your youth, when you were naked and bare and squirming in your blood. (Ezekiel 16:1-22, *New American Standard Bible*)

The parable describes God giving life to the nation of Israel. He not only gave her life, He gave her the best life. However, she

9. The Value of Right Relationships

was not satisfied with the goodness of God. She lusted after other gods; false priests and prophets, the most popular religious activity, and turned away from the truth of God. The Word of God is self-explanatory.

> How shall I pardon you for this? Your children have forsaken Me and sworn by those that are not gods. When I had fed them to the full, then they committed adultery and assembled themselves by troops in the harlots' houses. They were like well-fed lusty stallions; Every one neighed after his neighbor's wife. Shall I not punish them for these things?" says the LORD. And shall I not avenge Myself on such a nation as this? Go up on her walls and destroy, but do not make a complete end. Take away her branches, for they are not the LORD's. For the house of Israel and the house of Judah have dealt very treacherously with Me," says the LORD. They have lied about the LORD, and said, "It is not He. Neither will evil come upon us, nor shall we see sword or famine. And the prophets become wind, for the word is not in them. Thus shall it be done to them." (Jeremiah 5:7-13)

Israel's spiritual adultery brought devastation to the nation of Israel. In 586 B.C. the temple in Jerusalem was destroyed, but God had sent threats and warnings for over four hundred years. Through the centuries God was patient and said over and over again "return to Me" (Joel 2:12; Hosea 6:1; Isaiah 31:6; Jeremiah 3:11-14; Lamentations 3:40; Malachi 3:7). The consequence for spiritual adultery was ex-communication from the favorable presence of God.

The New Testament describes spiritual adultery in unmistakably clear terms. "Adulterers and adulteresses! Do you not know that friendship with the world is enmity with God? Whoever therefore wants to be a friend of the world makes himself an enemy of God" (James 4:4). Based on the evidence from the Bible and the history of the church, the people of God individually and the church collectively are guilty of the sin of spiritual adultery. Maybe most of the time has been and still is taken up with the judicial process of trials and punishment for physical adultery. Let the following statement be repeated. Adultery, spiritual and physical, is a sin against God. Both may be forgiven and neither is a damning sin if the sinner repents and returns to the Lord. Adultery in any form is the same as unfaithfulness in any form.

The remedy for physical adultery is leave, cleave and become one. The remedy for spiritual adultery is:

>Stop chasing every new religious idea.
>Stop trying to please God with ungodly gimmicks.
>Start seeking doctrinal purity.
>Start praying for the grace of repentance.
>Start practicing the biblical principle of humility.

Coram Deo!

10. The Value of a Sacred Trust

You shall not steal

Exodus 20:15

There is a close relationship between a sacred trust and the eighth commandment, "You shall not steal." God's endowment of every gift to the human being is a sacred trust. From the air you breathe to the ability to think is all a gift from God.

Christians tend to use the term Materialism to describe the attitude of this present consuming society. Actually what they really mean is consumerism. Materialism is a philosophical proposition that tries to define the existence of reality. Materialism argues for a universe that is not controlled by intelligence, but rather by some material source or power. Consumerism is a worldview that places worth and value to the consumption of goods. Consumerism is a god of this present world that demonstrates the proclivity to find happiness in the power of buying consumer goods. For instance consumerism finds satisfaction by purchasing a new home, a new vehicle, a new recreational toy, a new appliance, or even a new Bible. Author and pollster, George Barna, says, "The traditional American Dream…is being revised." It is being revised because Consumerism has failed in every area of life. Consumerism leaves behind misery and heartache along with unfathomable indebtedness. It failed because the American public has violated God's sacred trust. Consumerism is a violation of the eighth commandment, "You shall not steal."

The English word "steal" is translated from the Greek word *klepto* in the New Testament. It describes a passion for stealing by means of stealth and secrecy. You've heard of a kleptomaniac; The kleptomaniac never tells the store manager, "I've stolen several items from you today." The thief is always shrewd, clever, and secretive. The great thief of the world is Satan. Many professing Christians do not believe they have broken the eighth commandment. A good example is the young rich ruler and his brief encounter with Jesus Christ.

> Now behold, one came and said to Him, "Good Teacher, what good thing shall I do that I may have eternal life?" So He said to him, "Why do you call Me good? No one is good but One, that is, God. But if you want to enter into life, keep the commandments." He said to Him, "Which ones?" Jesus said, " 'You shall not murder,' 'You shall not commit adultery,' 'You shall not steal,' 'You shall not bear false witness,' 'Honor your father and your mother,' and, 'You shall love your neighbor as yourself.'" The young man said to Him, "All these things I have kept from my youth. What do I still lack?" Jesus said to him, "If you want to be perfect, go, sell what you have and give to the poor, and you will have treasure in heaven; and come, follow Me." But when the young man heard that saying, he went away sorrowful, for he had great possessions. (Matthew 19:16-22)

Either the young rich ruler was deluded and did not understand the law or Matthew captured the irony of his discourse. Maybe the young rich ruler had not heard the law expounded from Leviticus. "If one of your brethren becomes poor, and falls into poverty among you then you shall help him, like a stranger or a sojourner, that he may live with you" (Leviticus 25:35). This young man loved his possessions, but obviously he did not love the truth of the law. If he knew the law, he knew he was a thief. Like the inspired wisdom writer said, "What is desired in a man is kindness, and a poor man is better than a liar" (Proverbs 19:22). It is possible that the young man was unaware of his contradiction, as many people do contradict themselves, but Matthew used the irony under inspiration from God to teach us a lesson. The lesson is: Don't say you don't steal and then fail to obey the Lord who is the giver of all possessions.

Accumulating possessions is a passion for a major portion of the American society. All the physical stuff we possess will

10. The Value of a Sacred Trust

eventually wear out and we or our progeny will discard it. There is a commodity that will outlive us and all our heirs. It is called land. The word "land" is derived from the Hebrew word *eretz*. The word "land" is used in the English Bible over 1500 times. Sometimes the Bible uses the word land in the possessive case. It is found early and often.

Genesis 20:15 describes the time when Abraham visited Abimelech and Abraham was told by the king: "Behold my land is before you; settle where ever you please." "My land" implies ownership.

1 King 10:6 describes the Queen of Sheba visiting with Solomon: "It was a true report which I heard in my own land about your words and your wisdom." "My own land" is an explicit reference to ownership.

Land ownership and acquisition of wealth sounds like free enterprise and capitalism until you hear God on the issue of land ownership and loving wealth.

> Thus says the LORD: What injustice have your fathers found in Me, That they have gone far from Me, Have followed idols, And have become idolaters? Neither did they say, 'Where is the LORD, Who brought us up out of the land of Egypt, Who led us through the wilderness, Through a land of deserts and pits, Through a land of drought and the shadow of death, Through a land that no one crossed And where no one dwelt?' I brought you into a bountiful country, To eat its fruit and its goodness. But when you entered, you defiled My land And made My heritage an abomination. (Jeremiah 2:5-7)

It sure sounds like God has a deed to the property. The most precious commodity we have is land and yet no one really owns one acre. It all belongs to God. The Hebrew word *eretz* is also translated into another English word. It is earth. The word "earth" is found over 600 times in the Old Testament over 150 times in the New Testament. Also in the Old Testament the word *eretz* is translated "ground" 120 times. Although *eretz* is used figuratively, it primarily refers to dirt. The earth, the land, the ground, and the dirt are distinctively theocentric. That means God is central to all existence including the precious commodity called land. Think about what the Bible says about the earth:

God created it (Genesis 1:1).
God used it to design rational creatures and plants (Genesis 2:7-8).
God preserves it (Genesis 8:22).
God owns it (Psalm 24:1).
God will destroy it (Revelation 21:1).

This exercise and the Bible quotes are not intended to prove the wonderful attributes of God, but rather to show the need to understand the biblical principle of stewardship and how stewardship relates to the commandment, "You shall not steal."

Stewardship begins by recognizing God's power over all human possession. For instance, God gave the Israelites in the Old Testament specific laws regulating the acquisition and disposal of land. Listen carefully to the Word of God. "The land, moreover, shall not be sold permanently, for the land is Mine; for you are but aliens and sojourners with Me" (Leviticus 25:23). The principle of the Levitical text is that God owns the land forever. We are temporary managers of God's land.

The biblical principle of stewardship ought to be studied carefully and humbly, because of the sinful desire to possess things, and land being one of the most precious possessions. It may not be a sin to desire possessions, but it is a sin to desire possessions with an inordinate passion. God owns everything. God simply grants humans the privilege of having stewardship over them in this life.

The eighth commandment is most often violated as a sin against God, but it is a sin against other men and a sin against self. To steal is a universal temptation to all men. The commandment "You shall not steal" is habitually broken when we think that our possessions are more important than our relationship with God. Remember the young rich ruler and how Jesus felt a love for him, and said to him, "One thing you lack: go and sell all you possess, and give to the poor, and you shall have treasure in heaven; and come follow me" (Mark 10:17ff). The man was not willing to sell his property. He loved his property more that he loved Jesus Christ. This man broke the eighth commandment, because he was stealing from God. He was willing to sacrifice a favorable eternal relationship with God just to have his earthly possessions. This text in Mark is often misinterpreted by some TV evangelist who tries to overwhelm your emotions with guilt if you do not give to their cause. Interesting enough, they never follow the biblical mandate to give to the ministry of the local church. This text does not require anyone to sell their possessions unless those possessions are more important than God Himself. What the Lord does require is that you honor Him first in all things: In your worship, in your doctrine, in your practice, and in your stewardship. To do anything less is to steal from God.

There are many ways in which this commandment may be broken. Christians violate this law when they steal from God! Christians steal from God by not keeping the commandments found in the Word of God.

1. If you have other gods before the true and living God, you rob God of His rightful place in existence.
2. If you worship the true God in the wrong manner, you rob God by denying His sovereignty and dignity.
3. If you abuse and misuse the name of the Lord, you rob God of His distinctive and true character.
4. If you do not work hard six days, you rob God of His generous providence.
5. If you do not keep the Lord's day, you rob God of due worship.

The way to be a good steward is to obey all the commandments.

Christians steal from God by not using and managing their time wisely for His glory. Time is hard to define, however the biblical concept of time is a way to measure historical progress. Time may be measured because it has a beginning and an end. Eternity has no beginning and no end. God gives time; His creatures manage it. Time is a precious gift from God. Stealing from God by using time for selfish purposes is just as sinful as violating any of the other commandments.

Those things that God has entrusted to us for this brief lifetime come to us either by God's free gift or by our own labors. When Christians resort to theft they are stealing either from someone else or themselves. In either case, Christians who commit robbery violate some fundamental laws that regulate how Christians relate to one another. There are two laws that will help Christians understand this principle.

The first law necessary for good relationships is the law of love. Giving to someone is an expression of love. A robber cannot love the person from whom he steals from and the robbed must not love the person who stole from him.

The second law necessary for good relationships is the law of labor. The thief attempts to have someone else's possessions, therefore the thief steals the labor of the other person.

Stealing money or property from another person is a crime in the eyes of God whether the state says it is a crime or not. It may be robbery at gunpoint, but it may be robbery by deceit. The art of sophistry is the most common tool used by the thief to steal by deceit. Sophistry is when someone of alleged authority says something that is not true, but it sounds true and the person hearing it receives it as truth. The advertising industry is particularly guilty of breaking this commandment.

Robbery by default in a contract or a debt owed is typical in the American consuming society. It is particularly disgraceful when Christians default on a contract or fail to pay a debt.

Gambling is considered a virtue in this country. Dr. R. L. Dabney published the following argument in 1897. His argument is that gambling is theft and a violation of the eighth commandment. This brief quote from Dabney is biblically sound and rationally indisputable.

10. The Value of a Sacred Trust

To take your neighbor's property in a game of chance is theft, for you give no quid pro quo. Does one say that the loser surrenders his property voluntarily? The answer is that his consent is one which he has no right to give, because it is prompted by an immoral motive, namely: the hope of plundering his rival. Or is it argued that the loser receives his expected and his fair quid pro quo in his sport? I answer: This is false. That is not the quid pro quo which either winner or loser really has in view. The real aim of both is plunder - not the sport. This is proved by the question: Why, then, do they not play for the sport without the bets? Another element in the sin is the insincere, and therefore profane, appeal made to Divine Providence in the lot. Chance is no cause, as the gamester ought to know. But the real cause is Providence. The practical proof of the immorality of gaming is, that all habitual gamblers proceed from "fair gaming," sooner or later, to tricks which even their own code condemns as frauds. (*The Practical Philosophy*, by R. L. Dabney, p. 485)

There are many ways to steal from other people.

1. In connection with the sixth commandment Christians may rob a person of his or her good name by slander or telling something not true.

2. In connection with the seventh commandment Christians may rob a person of his or her dignity by committing adultery.

3. Christians violate this commandment by turning their backs on those in need. "Whoever has this world's goods, and sees his brother in need, and shuts up his heart from him, how does the love of God abide in him?" (1 John 3:17).

4. If Christians waste what God has provided through one of His servants, they break the eighth commandment.

5. People commonly rob from each other by way of neglect. For instance, if you open your car door and put a small dent or scratch the paint on the car next to yours, you have violated the eighth commandment unless you notify the owner of the other car and make appropriate arrangements. Your neglect caused a decrease in the value of the vehicle you damaged, thus it is theft.

6. In connection with the ninth commandment, one may be robbed of the truth and the gospel message by ignorant and ungodly pastors and elders in the church. This has been an ongoing plague beginning in the Old Testament church. "Thus says the LORD of hosts: 'Do not listen to the words of the prophets who prophesy to you. They make you worthless; they speak a vision of their own heart, not from the mouth of the LORD...I have not sent these prophets, yet they ran. I have not spoken to them yet they prophesied'" (Jeremiah 23:12-21). The false prophets were zealous, but there message was false. They were taking the people down the path into exile.

Francis Turretin's brief summary cuts to the marrow, relative to the eighth commandment.

> To theft belong also reductively all deceits, frauds, and overreaching in contracts, measures, weights, monies, monopolies and all evil arts and trickery by which another's property is appropriated. Yea, they are guilty of the theft in the sight of God who devote themselves to indolence and depraved ease (which is the cushion of the devil) and who, in their callings professions and ministries, are negligent and unfaithful - who unjustly steal the wages allowed them, performing lazily and imperfectly the work entrusted to them. (*Institutes of Elenctic Theology*, by Francis Turretin, vol. 2, p. 123)

Christians not only steal from God and their fellow man, but they may steal from themselves.

1. They rob themselves and their families by not providing the necessities of life.

2. They rob themselves and their families by squandering the estate that God has provided.

3. They rob themselves of the means of grace (preaching, sacraments, and prayer) by not worshiping God according to His Word.

4. They rob themselves of the joy of salvation by allowing the trials of life to turn into temptations and the temptations turn into sin.

The question to ask is why do Christians violate this commandment when they know better? Of course the basic answer is the sin nature. However there are specific reasons:

> Sinfulness causes Christians to misunderstand necessity
> Sinfulness causes Christians to be lazy
> The sin nature harbors greed and greed causes robbery
> Love of money
> Love of possessions
> The desire to be noticed
> The sin nature causes one not to trust God.

The commandment "You shall not steal" is habitually broken when Christians think that God will not supply their needs.

The biblical promise is, "God shall supply all your needs according to His riches in glory by Christ Jesus" (Philippians 4:19). This promise teaches the Christian to be content with God's generous providence and to seek gain honestly and lawfully for the glory of God. If anyone violates this commandment does it mean eternal damnation for that person? It depends on the state of the soul. Obviously the soul marked by the righteous of Jesus Christ is eternally secure. However, the soul marked by the righteousness of Jesus Christ will have the desire to live by the righteousness of Jesus

Christ. Sanctification will progressively mature the Christian so that he or she will be less inclined to violate this commandment.

A question often asked is, "Why do the dishonest prosper?" Can it truly be said that the wicked, dishonest thieves prosper? They may have more possessions in this life than the poor child of God, but is that prosperity? There can be no prosperity without pleasure and all real pleasure comes from God.

The Psalmist says this about the wicked prosperous man. "I have seen the wicked in great power, And spreading himself like a native green tree. Yet he passed away, and behold, he was no more; Indeed I sought him, but he could not be found. Mark the blameless man, and observe the upright; For the future of that man is peace" (Psalm 37:35-37).

Christians must remember that the Lord was sinless. He never stole anything. But when the Lord was crucified, He was crucified among thieves. He was not merely between two thieves; He hung on the cross bearing shame and guilt for sinful thieves. When we see our own theft and find ourselves among thieves, remember how the Lord looked upon them.

The possessions that God places in your care are a sacred trust. How you maintain it and manage it reflects your attitude toward God. No matter how hard you try, you fall short of the glory of God with this commandment.

If you confess that you've violated the eighth commandment you have taken the first step to find grace, mercy and forgiveness. Like the thief on the cross, you must trust Christ and Christ alone. For Christ is a sacred trust above all the possessions you may acquire in this life.

Thieves must look to Jesus Christ, the spotless Lamb of God for redemption. It is the thief who understands the gravity of these words: "Today you shall be with me in Paradise."

11. The Value of Truth

You shall not bear false witness against your neighbor.
Exodus 20:16

The Hebrew text literally says, "Do not give false testimony against your neighbor." The commandment may sound narrow in its scope and application, until one inquires into the full counsel of God. As with all the commandments, there is a negative and positive dimension. The negative dimension in children's language is "do not lie." The positive dimension is "tell the truth." Consulting the full counsel of God reveals the fundamental principle of the ninth commandment. The principle doctrine found in the ninth commandment relates to truth and how God's moral law demands truth.

The words "do not give false testimony" is best understand in terms of legal language. This reflects the legal process used in Israel in which a person is expected to give a response at a trial. If the court calls someone to testify, the testimony is under oath and nothing but the truth is the standard. We are all on trial to give truthful testimony and God is the Judge.

The ninth commandment requires a person to tell the truth about his or her neighbor. The immediate question is: Who is my neighbor? We must consider the word neighbor in the larger context. When the Pharisees asked the question, "Who is my neighbor?", Jesus responded with the parable of the good Samaritan (Luke 10:25-37). "You shall love your neighbor as yourself" (Leviticus 19:18; Matthew 22:39) and has no relational limitations. Your neighbor is the person who comes your way according to the providence of God.

Throughout this exposition of the Ten Commandments, I have alleged that the world of communication technology has changed the way people think. It has been said that we are living in the fastest age in human history. We know that time is not relative.

The measurement for time is consistent. There are 60 minutes for each hour, etc and it always has been. What is different is what we can accomplish in those 60 minutes compared to a few generations ago. For instance, no one would travel very far out of the community for regular worship services and church related activities. Now days it is not uncommon for people to drive to different towns or communities to associate with a local church. Human history is moving at the same pace it has always moved. However, with the speed and flow of information, the acquisition of information is faster than it has ever been before.

Telephone (FAXs), radio, television and computer networks have greatly enhanced the ability to instantaneously communicate ideas. We must not denigrate the positive dimensions of electronic communications, but on the other hand, we must not ignore the negative factors of electronic communications.

Radio has a variety of music, talk shows, preachers and teachers with their own programs. Many of them promote anti-intellectual agendas with a wide variety of very different biblical doctrines. Television, video, and smart phones have the same influence, but the visual elements corrupt or maybe even destroy the thinking process.

On top of all this, we live in the postmodern era. Many Ivy League colleges teach literary deconstructionism as the accepted method for interpreting human language. Deconstructionism teaches that the author uses words to compose a literary piece, but those words are meaningless to the recipient until someone deconstructs the words and gives them meaning. This means there is no absolute truth for any written communication. To put it another way the author had no real intention to convey absolute truth with the words. The ninth commandment must be understood based on two inseparable biblical concepts. They are human communication and truth.

Do Americans believe there is absolute truth? George Barna, a Christian author and pollster has conducted several surveys to determine the way Americans think of truth. In a 2002 poll of 1,002 adults only 44% of born-again adults are certain that absolute

11. The Value of Truth

moral truth exists. Only 9% of born-again teenagers believe in absolute moral truth. In August 2005 the Barna Research Group reported that 35% believe that moral truth is absolute. The ninth commandment commands and demands the communication of truth. Why are professing Christians becoming less inclined to believe in absolute truth?

They are disinclined to believe the first eight commandments.
They are inclined to believe there are many gods.
They do not believe the true God requires true worship.
They do not have the proper reverence for God.
They do not work and worship according to God's commandments.
They do not respect the authority of God.
They do not value life or property.
They do not place any value on truth.

Most of what Christians read, hear, and see is fantasy, therefore the truth of reality does not satisfy the human lust for power and excitement. Christians understand truth and practice truth telling to be effective witnesses of God's grace. The Bible teaches us that the church is the pillar and foundation of truth (1 Timothy 3:15). Truth transcends time and cultures despite the false witness by many professing Christians that truth is culturally relative. The Psalmist put it in these terms: "For His lovingkindness is great toward us, and the truth of the Lord is everlasting" (Psalm 117:2).

The Word of God speaks of the ninth commandment clearly, intelligently, and often.

> Exodus 23:1 "You shall not circulate a false report. Do not put your hand with the wicked to be an unrighteous witness."
>
> Exodus 23:7 "Keep yourself far from a false matter... ."
>
> Leviticus 6:2 "If a person sins and commits a trespass against the LORD by lying to his neighbor... ."

Leviticus 19:16 "You shall not go about as a talebearer among your people... ."

Psalm 5:6 "You shall destroy those who speak falsehood..."

Psalm 58:3 "They go astray as soon as they are born, speaking lies... ."

This commandment practically necessitates the use of words to obey it or to abuse it. The use of true words and the misuse of false words have serious consequences under certain circumstances. The unforgivable sin is a prominent example (Matthew 12:31-32). It requires words to commit the unforgivable sin.

It all started a long time ago. In fact, when Satan told the woman "You will not surely die" she believed the lie (Genesis 3:4). It caused the death of a favorable relationship with God for the entire human race. Since that time people have lied to God, to each other and to themselves. For thousands of years the human race has been busy, working hard, to "suppress the truth" (Romans 1:18). They have "exchanged the truth of God for a lie" (Romans 1:25).

The nation of Israel in the Old Testament consisted of God's people; they professed, professed, and professed to be God's people. They had seen the fall of 10 tribes of the northern kingdom. For nearly 600 years God sent one messenger of truth after the other. When Israel was about to fall into the hands of the great King Nebuchadnezzar and taken into exile, the Lord prophesied through the prophet Jeremiah.

Jeremiah 7:10 "Truth has perished and has been cut off from their mouth."

Jeremiah 8:5 "They hold fast to deceit."

Jeremiah 8:8 "Look, the false pen of the scribe certainly works falsehood."

11. The Value of Truth

Jeremiah 8:10 "From the prophet even to the priest everyone deals falsely."

The prophets were the teachers in Israel. They were supposed to teach the truth, but falsehood came out of their mouth. They were clinging to their deceptive teaching, perhaps thinking they could deceive God. The scribe copied the law accompanied by the false presumption that Israel kept the law. Finally God said, "like preacher, like pew." To put it another way the Old Testament congregation had listened to the lies of the prophet for so long, they actually believed the lies. The truth of God's holiness and promises had been lost. The truth that man was a sinner and needed to repent, had been lost. The next step was awful. God gave them what they wanted: to live among the pagans like the pagans.

Now fast-forward 600 years to find Jesus Christ, the son of the true God, in a confrontation with the heirs of the Old Testament church. The Jewish religious leaders, known by the name Pharisees, suggested that Jesus was born of fornication. Then Jesus told them that God was His Father. The rest of the truth that came from the mouth of Jesus was a declaration that fills the ninth commandment with meat for every generation of Christians to chew on and digest. Professing Christians who are not interested in understanding truth ought to read these words from Jesus

> Why do you not understand My speech? Because you are not able to listen to My word. You are of your father the devil, and the desires of your father you want to do. He was a murderer from the beginning, and does not stand in the truth, because there is no truth in him. When he speaks a lie, he speaks from his own resources, for he is a liar and the father of it. But because I tell the truth, you do not believe Me. Which of you convicts Me of sin? And if I tell the truth, why do you not believe Me? He who is of God hears God's words; therefore you do not hear, because you are not of God. (John 8:43-47)

The words of truth did not fall on the ears of the Old Testament church in 586 B.C. or in 30 A.D. The wisdom writer rightly said, "death and life are in the power of the tongue" (Proverbs 18:21). It was death for the Old Testament church, because the prophets (preachers and teachers) did not realize the value of truth. Truth is life in Jesus Christ, because He is the truth. The discovery and testimony of truth is the duty and privilege for every Christian.

The standard for Christians to measure truth is the Word of God. The Psalmist says, "The sum of Thy word is truth" (Psalm 119.160). If the Bible is right, and it is, then the ultimate standard for truth is the mind of God. The Bible reveals the mind of God for the benefit of the creature, but reserves unfathomable mysteries that will be revealed in glory. Our private moral judgments do not count unless they line up with the Word of God.

Jesus said, "from within, out of the heart of men, proceed evil thoughts, adulteries, fornication's, murders, thefts, covetousness, wickedness, and deceit" (Matthew 15:19). The Bible also says, "The heart is deceitful above all things" (Jeremiah 17:9). Words and actions reflect the condition of the heart.

I have heard people say, "I'd never tell a lie!" It is a sign of either ignorance or arrogance. It may be ignorance because of a limited understanding of the biblical teaching on the subject of falsehood and truth. It is arrogant for anyone to believe he or she is without sin. The apostle Peter is a good example. He was standing outside in the courtyard waiting to the see the outcome of the trial of the Lord Jesus Christ. It was just a few hours before that Peter had told the Lord "Even if I have to die with You, I will not deny You." A young slave girl accused Peter saying, "You also were with Jesus of Galilee" and Peter denied it saying, "I do not know the man" (Matthew 26:69-75). Peter broke the ninth commandment three times within a few hours. When I hear someone say, "I'd never tell a lie" I think of Peter's lie to Jesus Christ.

Christians owe God the truth. King David gave his son Solomon final instructions during the transfer of leadership to King Solomon. Truth was at the forefront of those instructions.

11. The Value of Truth

> And keep the charge of the LORD your God: to walk in His ways, to keep His statutes, His commandments, His judgments, and His testimonies, as it is written in the Law of Moses, that you may prosper in all that you do and wherever you turn; that the LORD may fulfill His word which He spoke concerning me, saying, "If your sons take heed to their way, to walk before Me in truth with all their heart and with all their soul," He said, "you shall not lack a man on the throne of Israel." (1 Kings 2:3-4)

Solomon's offspring stopped walking before God in truth and God stopped walking with them. Four hundred years later they were captured by the Babylonians and served as slaves. Ananias and Sapphira thought they could deceive God. There were deadly consequences.

> But a certain man named Ananias, with Sapphira his wife, sold a possession. And he kept back part of the proceeds, his wife also being aware of it, and brought a certain part and laid it at the apostles' feet. But Peter said, "Ananias, why has Satan filled your heart to lie to the Holy Spirit and keep back part of the price of the land for yourself? While it remained, was it not your own? And after it was sold, was it not in your own control? Why have you conceived this thing in your heart? You have not lied to men but to God." Then Ananias, hearing these words, fell down and breathed his last. So great fear came upon all those who heard these things. (Acts 5:1-5)

Christians ought to study and understand the doctrine of truth, so they may be truthful in their relationship with their neighbor. God has given His people specific instructions that need to be on every Christians "to do" list. These are the things you shall do: "Speak each man the truth to his neighbor; Give judgment in your gates for truth, justice, and peace; Let none of you think evil in your heart against your neighbor; And do not love a false oath. For all these are things that I hate," says the LORD" (Zechariah 8:16). God does hate. The Bible says so on many occasions and the Bible is not a liar. The book of Proverbs is very clear (See Proverbs 6:17-19). These six things the LORD hates, Yes, seven are an abomination to Him:

1. A proud look
2. A lying tongue
3. Hands that shed innocent blood
4. A heart that devises wicked plans
5. Feet that are swift in running to evil
6. A false witness who speaks lies
7. And one who sows discord among brethren

God hates unrighteousness and lying is unrighteousness. Satan will try to deceive you with his charm and speak to your soul, just like he did to Eve and say, "surely God does not hate liars." The Holy Spirit of God speaking from the Word of God responds: "all liars shall have their part in the lake which burns with fire and brimstone..." (Revelation 21:8). There is hope, in fact a promise to all liars, from God: "Repent and believe in the gospel" and "you will be saved" (Mark 1:5; Acts 16:31). Only the righteousness of Jesus Christ can save a liar.

Then what constitutes a lie? The answer is simple: Anything contrary to the truth is a lie. Many professing Christians are not outright liars, but they are subtle liars. Every false statement is a lie. Although there are too many examples to list, a few will suffice. An unconditional promise not fulfilled is a lie. If someone says "I will do such and such tomorrow" and someone fails to carry out the promise, it is a lie. The fallible human mind is incapable of making a future promise without adding a suffix to it. *Deo volente*, or Lord willing, ought to accompany every promise to our neighbor.

God ordains intervening historical contingencies that may prevent someone from fulfilling a promise. Then the promise breaker (the liar) must seek forgiveness from the other party and from God.

11. The Value of Truth

False preachers and teachers are liars. Teaching the Word of God is a noble and necessary enterprise in the Christian religion. However, "my brethren let not many of you become teachers, know that we shall receive a stricter judgment" (James 3:1). Preachers and teachers must ultimately preach and teach the truth, "not as pleasing to men, but God who tests our hearts" (1 Thessalonians 2:4). Peter describes false teachers in terms of being "like natural brute beasts made to be caught and destroyed, speak evil of the things they do not understand, and will utterly perish in their own corruption, and will receive the wages of unrighteousness, as those who count it pleasure to carouse in the daytime. They are spots and blemishes, carousing in their own deceptions while they feast with you..." (2 Peter 2:12-13). The obvious truth is the evangelical church overflows with false teachers. For instance, when one preacher or teacher says the Bible teaches a particular doctrine (you fill in the blank) and another preacher or teacher says the Bible teaches the opposite, then you have a contradiction. One or the other of them is not telling the truth. Doctrinal indifference is eating away the once strong church in North America. Restore the truth in the pulpit and God may be gracious and merciful to the wayward evangelical church.

Slander and gossip are lies. "He who goes about as a slanderer reveals secrets, Therefore do not associate with a gossip" (Proverbs 20:19). Wisdom from the Word of God is this: stay away from liars.

The *Westminster Larger Catechism* (question 144) defines the duties required to obey this commandment:

> Promoting the truth between man and man,
> Appearing and standing for truth,
> Speak the truth in matters of judgment and justice,
> Unwilling to admit of an evil report,
> Discouraging talebearers, flatterers, and slanderers,
> Keeping all lawful promises,

Studying and practicing of whatsoever things are true, honest, lovely, and of good report.

The *Westminster Larger Catechism* (Question 145) also defines the sins forbidden in this commandment:

Preserve the good name of our neighbor,
Giving false evidence,
Reward the wicked according to the work of the righteous,
Holding our peace when iniquity calls for a reproof,
Misrepresenting intentions, words, and actions,
Thinking too highly of one's self,
Raising false rumors,
Breach of lawful promises,
Countenancing evil reports,
Speaking the truth unseasonably, or maliciously to a wrong end or perverting the truth into a wrong meaning,

The doctrine associated with the ninth commandment is derived from the whole counsel of God; it is exceedingly wide and very deep. There are two doctrinal principles derived from a study of the ninth commandment.

The first principle is that where there is a lie on the tongue, Satan is in the heart. Professing Christians allow Satan to deceive them into believing that truth is relative to circumstances, conditions, and cultures. Christians who reject the truth will be drawn into the vortex of Satan's lies. For too long truth and error have slept comfortably in the same bed.

The second principle is that for those who have violated this commandment, there is refuge in the righteousness of the one who is the Truth, the Lord Jesus Christ. Run to Him, confess, repent, ask forgiveness and be restored into the joy of God's saving grace.

12. The Law of Contentment

You shall not covet your neighbor's house; you shall not covet your neighbor's wife, nor his male servant, nor his female servant, nor his ox, nor his donkey, nor anything that is our neighbor's.

Exodus 20:17

There is a sense in which all sins can be traced to three root sins. They are pride, lust and covetousness. Those three root sins have mutual connections. They are all factors in the fall of the human race. Many theologians from various Christian churches agree that covetousness is the queen of all sins.

The Hebrew word translated "covet" or "desire" carries with it the idea of a passionate pleasure. Not necessarily just sexual lust or an unfulfilled appetite of some sort, but any inordinate desire to have something that God has chosen not to supply at a particular time.

God created Adam and Eve and gave them a perfect world. They had no reason to covet anything, but the sin of covetousness was irresistible. Eve coveted the thing that God prohibited. "So when the woman saw that the tree was good for food, that it was pleasant to the eyes, and a tree desirable to make one wise, she took of its fruit and ate" (Genesis 3:6). Satan convinced Eve she could be "like God" (Genesis 3:5). The tree was desirable. The word desirable from the Hebrew word *chamad* is the same Hebrew word translated "covet" in Exodus 20:17.

The history of the human race, from empires to cities, from rich and the poor, is a history of congested covetousness. After the flood, some of Noah's descendents coveted "a name" which implies equality with God (Genesis 11:4). After God delivered His people from slavery in Egypt, the Old Testament church "yielded to intense craving" for the food back in Egypt (Numbers 11:4). During the conquest Achan coveted "gold and silver" (Joshua 7:21). God gave David a kingdom along with all the amenities that accompany royalty. Like Eve, he saw a desirable object that was off-limits, but David coveted a very beautiful naked woman (2 Samuel 11:2-4).

Although there are too many examples of covetousness to mention, an event that preceded the fall of the northern kingdom in 722 B.C. and the fall of Jerusalem in 586 B.C. is worthy of attention. The prophet Micah warned of the coming disaster by preaching against the sins that provoked God's wrath. Micah was a prophet during the time that the Northern Kingdom of Israel was under siege by the Assyrians. In 722 B. C. the Northern Kingdom of Israel fell into the hands of the Assyrians.

Micah has been called "the conscience of Israel" because his message revealed the moral and social evils of his time. His preaching must have been very powerful. Nearly 100 years after the time of Micah the prophet Jeremiah mentioned Micah's ministry. Jeremiah said Micah prophesied in the days of Hezekiah the king of Judah. Micah was very likely part of the revival and reformation that took place during Hezekiah's rule. Micah's ministry spanned over a period between 40 and 50 years. During that time there were national and international events that kept Israel in upheaval.

In spite of the political intrigue and rebellion against God, Israel prospered economically and commercially. Corruption, bribery, and conspiracy prevailed rather than justice and respect for God's law. Material prosperity eclipsed the source of wealth and material blessings.

The threat from surrounding nations, especially Assyria's imminent invasion, paled in significance to the internal turmoil that eventually turned into anarchy.

Micah delivered his message to all God's covenant people, then known as the nation Israel, now known as the church. Micah charged God's covenant people with evil plotting, covetousness, oppression and false prophecy. From the prophets mouth the words inspired by God should have been sufficient warning to those who professed to be children of God. "Woe to those who devise iniquity, and work out evil on their beds! At morning light they practice it, because it is in the power of their hand. They covet fields and take them by violence, also houses, and seize them. So they oppress a man and his house, a man and his inheritance" (Micah 2:1-2).

The people of Judah and Jerusalem professed to have God as their Father, so they were related to one another because of God's grace. They were like brothers and sisters. They should have treated each other with equity and compassion. However, they were plotting evil against one another. Some translations say they were devising evil against one another. In either case it was deliberate planning. Micah implies that it was the wealthy upper class oppressing the poor lower class. "It is in the power of their hand" to steal property and houses.

The root sin was covetousness. Micah preached against injustice, oppression, fraud, and corruption. Covetousness was the root of all these sins. They were never happy with God's bountiful provision. Our time is not much different than Micah's time. Christians are fascinated with power and wealth.

Now is the time to have a *kairotic* moment in your spiritual experience. The first commandment is, "You shall have no other gods before Me." If you obey the first commandment, you will naturally obey the tenth commandment. If God is number one in your life, then it is not possible to break the remaining nine commandments. The tenth commandment is, "You shall not covet." It is not possible to covet, if you have God, because you will have everything. If you are perfectly content with what God has given you there would be no desire to break the previous nine commandments. It is called a *kairotic* moment because it is the high point of understanding the relationship these commandments have with each other.

The tenth commandment is the unseen condition of the heart. To put it another way, it is an inward problem. Covetousness is a condition of the mind, will and affections. In vulgar everyday language it is commonly called greed. It is the desire to have what you do not need.

Covetousness will be accompanied with an inordinate love for self, which is the mark of fallen men. Paul said men will be lovers of self (2 Timothy 3:2). An inordinate love for self and covetousness reflects a useless mind. Paul explains that "God gave them over to a debased mind, to do those things which are not fitting: being filled with all unrighteousness, sexual immorality, wickedness, covetousness, and maliciousness..." (Romans 1:28-29).

Covetousness is an inclination that stands ready to motivate murder, engage in immoral sex, steal and join the company of liars. If someone desires the reputation of another man and incapable of having a good reputation, then one person slanders the other to raise his or her own ego. All because they covet something they do not have. Greed is often the cause of sexual sins. People steal because the heart covets the things of this world. Some people will not discipline themselves to think intelligently, so they tell lies to try and impress people, because they covet attention.

The Bible teaches the source of everyone's sin. "Each one is tempted when he is drawn away by his own desires" (James 1:14). Every man is drawn away because of his own covetousness. It is not someone else that caused the coveting. James stresses individual responsibility.

The inspired writers of Holy Scripture associated covetousness with the most evil practices known to men. "Do you not know that the unrighteous will not inherit the kingdom of god? Do not be deceived. Neither fornicators, nor idolaters, nor adulterers, nor homosexuals, nor sodomites, nor thieves, nor covetous, nor drunkards, nor revilers, nor extortionist will inherit the kingdom of God" (1 Corinthians 6:9). Most people would say, "I would never do those evil things." Perhaps some people will not do some of those evil things, but what about the sin of covetousness? Remember covetousness is a heart sin. It is the desire that leads to the practical outworking of any sin.

Covetousness is not only a heart sin that leads to sinful human relationships, but covetousness has the potential to drive a wedge between man and God as it did in the Garden of Eden. The Psalmist said, "the wicked boasts of his heart's desire; he blesses the greedy and renounces the LORD" (Psalm 10:3). The covetous man curses and rejects the Lord. The covetous man is not content with God's promises, so he turns his back on God, which is the same as cursing and rejecting. The covetous man does what is right in his own eyes.

In one survey the Barna group indicated that 53% of the adult Christians surveyed claimed they did not violate the tenth commandment. Christians should examine the commandment "Thy shall not covet" in light of the whole teaching of Scripture to see if that 53% sounds like an accurate figure.

The Lord speaking through Jeremiah the prophet spoke these words to covetous Judah: "And do you seek great things for yourself? Do not seek them; for behold, I will bring adversity on all flesh" (Jeremiah 45:5). Judah had set her mind on the things of this world just like the church today. The thoughts of a covetous man are always seeking the things of this world. Too often there is more self-interest than there is God-interest. There is more emphasis on "my doctrine" than there is "biblical doctrine." There is more investment in a church building than in the heavenly home.

The Lord made it clear to the Old Testament church and the New Testament church should learn from it that seeking great things in this world is ridiculous, because everything in this world will eventually be destroyed. The covetous man takes great pain to gain the things of this world and cares little, if any, about eternal life and the heavenly home. The covetous man spends his time talking about this world. The covetous man is more interested in the business world, the sports world, the recreation world, and in short his own world than the world to come. The clergyman like the business man is concerned about worldly business and not about God's business.

A covetous man will not have an appetite for his spiritual estate. Prayer, the preaching of the Word of God, and the Sacraments do not appeal to him, because they speak to the soul not the body. Preachers ought to preach to the soul so that the heart may find heaven; but where covetousness is predominant, it chains men and women to the earth.

Why are Christians so easily deceived by the sin of covetousness? Probably because the law of contentment has been ignored for several generations of Christians. Contentment may be a blessing or the lack of contentment may be a curse. Paul explains in his inspired letter to Timothy.

> Now godliness with contentment is great gain. For we brought nothing into this world, and it is certain we can carry nothing out. And having food and clothing, with these we shall be content. But those who desire to be rich fall into temptation and a snare, and into many foolish and harmful lusts which drown men in destruction and perdition. For the love of money is a root of all kinds of evil, for which some have strayed from the faith in their greediness, and pierced themselves through with many sorrows. (1 Timothy 6:6-10)

Contentment is a virtue everyone should seek, but it seems that so few find it. The greatest enemy to contentment is prosperity. It appears that prosperity is one of the most dangerous trials a Christian will face; the church even more so. Prosperity inclines professing Christians to neglect God. Prosperity seems to tempt men with pride and arrogance rather than move them to repentance and humility.

There are remedies when tempted by prosperity. The first is humility. "You younger men, likewise, be subject to your elders; and all of you, clothe yourselves with humility toward one another, for God is opposed to the proud, but gives grace to the humble" (1 Peter 5:5). Prayer for God's provision and thanksgiving for His generous providence is a sure way to defeat the covetousness for prosperity. Live a moderate life neither self indulging or depriving oneself of necessities. Finally if God grants prosperity, use it for the kingdom of God

Christians must learn and re-learn the lesson given by inspiration from the Apostle Paul. "I have learned in whatever state I am, to be content" (Philippians 4:11). He understood as we should understand that God's grace is sufficient. Everyone alike is not endowed with the same gifts, talents, abilities, and portions in this life. Whatever God gives His children is sufficient for their needs and God's glory.

Christians should covet their spiritual relationship with their Creator, Provider, and Judge. Rather than coveting the benefits from this world they should continually seek to know God and make Him known.

The instructions from Scripture are clear. "For whatever is born of God overcomes the world. And this is the victory that has overcome the world - our faith. Who is he who overcomes the world, but he who believes that Jesus is the Son of God" (1 John 5:5).

Only one man has overcome the sin of covetousness - the Lord Jesus Christ. Our only hope is to believe that Jesus is the Son of God through faith alone. We must cry out like the disciples "Lord increase our faith" (Luke 17:5).

If Christians really believe, they ought to be challenging the culture and the church by calling men and women to repentance. Rather than coveting praise, money, pleasure, and success in this secular world, Christians should cry out, "Lord increase our faith." Lord, help us to be content with our lot in this life.

The law of God should be your delight. The child of God truly endeavors to keep God's law, because the child of God loves the lawgiver, the Lord Jesus Christ. Not if, but when God's children fail to perfectly keep God's law, then turn to the one who kept it perfectly. You will find perfection in the keeper of the law, the Lord Jesus Christ.

13. Where do we go Now?

After the death of Moses the servant of the LORD, it came to pass that the LORD spoke to Joshua the son of Nun, Moses' assistant, saying: "Moses My servant is dead. Now therefore, arise, go over this Jordan, you and all this people, to the land which I am giving to them—the children of Israel. Every place that the sole of your foot will tread upon I have given you, as I said to Moses. From the wilderness and this Lebanon as far as the great river, the River Euphrates, all the land of the Hittites, and to the Great Sea toward the going down of the sun, shall be your territory. No man shall be able to stand before you all the days of your life; as I was with Moses, so I will be with you. I will not leave you nor forsake you. Be strong and of good courage, for to this people you shall divide as an inheritance the land which I swore to their fathers to give them. Only be strong and very courageous, that you may observe to do according to all the law which Moses My servant commanded you; do not turn from it to the right hand or to the left, that you may prosper wherever you go. This Book of the Law shall not depart from your mouth, but you shall meditate in it day and night, that you may observe to do according to all that is written in it. For then you will make your way prosperous, and then you will have good success. Have I not commanded you? Be strong and of good courage; do not be afraid, nor be dismayed, for the LORD your God is with you wherever you go."

(Joshua 1:1-9)

"Wait a minute! You've made a wrong turn," my wife warned me as the highway suddenly became dirt road. The map indicated a good hard surface road. How could this happen? The road was supposed to be a short cut and we were already behind schedule. We came to an intersection a little further along the road. Mary turned to me with a smile and said, "where do we go now?"

Life is one intersection after another. Each intersection is potentially dangerous. A wrong turn may be a rough road or maybe worse, a dead end. "Where do we go now?" This is the question we all ask at one time or another. As Christians, we realize the itinerant nature of our lives. We are transient people with hope of a happy and joyful destination. The road map will direct us to the final destination, but many transitions will occur on the way. If Forest Gump wrote this he might say, "life is like a kaleidoscope." A little turn here and a little turn there will bring lots of changes.

The story of Israel's exit from Egypt and their wanderings and failures are all too familiar. God opened the Red Sea, gave the people food, and kept them from perishing when they did not deserve any better. Every event involved a choice, moving the people closer to the Promised Land. Today Christians are looking for God to open the Red Sea, when they would do well to look at the choices they face on a day to day basis. We must focus on the goal which is to be with God in the land He has promised us, the New Heavens and the New Earth.

God gave Moses the responsibility to lead the nation of Israel out of Egypt to the Promised Land. God called Moses to make godly choices. Before prophets became popular, Moses was the greatest prophet. In the absence of a king, Moses assumed responsibility for a nation of people. Moses was a gifted man, but he was not a military man. Moses appointed Joshua to choose an army to fight the battles for Israel. Joshua was like General Schwarzkopf, he was a military strategist. The really big transition for the nation of Israel was the shift of leadership from Moses to Joshua. All the wisdom, savvy, management ability, and experience of Moses was the trade off for a military man. A major transition period for the nation of Israel, but the goal remained the same. The people must take possession of the land that God promised to give them. When Joshua assumed command did the people ask, "where do we go now?" They probably did ask the question and probably with a sense of anxiety.

Most of us have seen Presidents of our nation come and go. The change of national leadership may cause a sense of anxiety because we wonder about our role in the world state of affairs. When your pastor announces that he will resign after twenty years at your church, there is probably a sense of anxiety. Wait a minute! Do not take the wrong turn at the intersection. Listen to what God says in His Word so you will make a godly choice.

God's promise to Joshua is a promise to you. "No man shall be able to stand before you all the days of your life; as I was with Moses, so I will be with you. I will not leave you nor forsake you" (Joshua 1:5).

After my conversion to Christianity late in life, I wanted everyone to know the forgiveness, acceptance, and peace I sensed from God. The Christian experience was not a fantasy. I knew that my experience was grounded in reality. What I did not know was whether or not God's promises were applicable to me? What about Joshua? Did he know that God's promises were applicable to him? What about you?

Immediately following the transition from Moses to Joshua God made a promise to Joshua. God said, "No one will be able to stand up against you all the days of your life. As I was with Moses, so I will be with you. I will never leave you nor forsake you" (Joshua 1:5). Wow! You mean God said He would never leave or forsake Joshua. Yes, not only Joshua, but God also makes that promise to you. God's children need to be constantly reminded of God's presence. As you face choices in this life the assurance of God's presence and His promises will sustain you.

Think back through this past week or this past year. Did you encounter some bumps in the road? Maybe a death in the family, a serious illness, a financial setback or at the very least a flat tire which made you late for an appointment was your bump in the road. Was God with you through the transition? Sure He was, or you would not be reading these words. Joshua was reminded of the previous faithfulness of God. God was with Moses during some difficult transitions and Moses was aware of God's presence. How many times does Moses refer to "the God of Abraham, Issac, and Jacob?" Too many to mention, but the point is that God is not just the God of three generations. He is the God of all generations. It was a reminder to Moses that God was with all previous generations, because God is an eternal God. The eternality of God is our benchmark to look back and see how God carried us through the transitions of life.

We live in a fast paced world, a technical world, and an image producing world. These characteristics do not serve well to remind us of God's presence. So, you may ask, how can I be reminded of God's past faithfulness? More particularly how will God's past faithfulness affect my present circumstances?

First, make sure there is oneness between you and God. The first step to oneness is, in the words of the Apostle Paul, "believe and you will be saved." Ask the Holy Spirit to empower you to follow the ways of the Lord. Then devote yourself to not only reading the Scriptures, but study the Scriptures.

Read church history and do not think for one minute that you will not be as spiritual as the next person. God promises to help us make godly choices. The evidence from those choices can be seen over and over again in nearly two thousand years of church history. The failure of the evangelical church to teach church history within the agenda of Christian Education robs Christianity of the great revivals and reformations. To ignore nearly two thousand years of church history will create a vacuum in the demonstrated promises of God. Do not deprive yourself of the joy of seeing how God has provided for and protected His children throughout the history of the church.

You can be reminded of God's faithfulness by pausing each day and giving thanks for an abundance of blessings. And for sure, ponder those choices you experienced and overcame by the grace of God! Write them in a journal, because next week, next month, or next year you will need to be reminded of God's faithfulness.

Most of us make it through transitions and say, "thank goodness it's over." During my undergraduate studies at Columbia International University, I had the opportunity to become friends with many married students. A married student with a couple of children taking a full load was likely to face financial difficulties at one time or another. I remember one student telling me that he was thankful for God's gracious hand as he went through some difficult times. He was quick to add that his primary concern was the future of his education. We are all thankful for God's gracious promises, but most of us come face to face choices with urgency about the future. Do you sometimes have that feeling that the road up ahead has some big bumps? Do you wonder how you will make it over those bumps?

God told Joshua, "I will be with you." The Hebrew verb translated "will be" refers to a future action as good as accomplished. It's like your favorite basketball team leading by thirty one points with only thirty seconds left in the game. You could say "we've won the game." When God called Moses to the task of leading the Israelites out of Egypt, God promised, "to bring them up from that land to a good and spacious land" (Exodus 3:8). God's plan did not change no matter how many roadblocks the Israelites would face or how difficult they may be. For the Israelites in the Old Testament and the Christians in the New Testament, and that includes you, God's great promise is His special and gracious presence. During the teenage years there will be an outburst of decisions. As teenagers become young adults new responsibilities bring more choices. When a single person becomes engaged and marriage takes place, then you have big-time choices. If your unmarried daughter announces she is pregnant, or your homosexual son comes out of the closet, or you lose you mate, then you are facing those choices in life that you thought would happen to the other person. When the choices come, and they will, remember God's past promises are also future promises. Trust Him today for the rest of your life. The words of the Psalmist are present tense as he says, "To you, O Lord, I lift up my soul; in you I trust, O my God" (Psalm 25:1-2). The Psalmist also looks to the future with positive expectations as he says, "When I am afraid, I will trust in you" (Psalm 56:3).

There is God's power for God's people to make godly choices. God told Joshua to "be strong and of good courage." To make sure Joshua understood God said, "Only be strong and very courageous" (Joshua 1:6-7).

My Father was a brick mason and during my teenage years I would work with him to earn extra money. My job was to mix mortar and keep him with a supply of brick. Needless to say, he was always calling for brick and mortar. The work was hard and taxing, even for a young body. One summer day near the end of the week I told my dad that I was about to give out. I remember him saying, "Its O.K. to give out, but don't give up." Sometimes Christians are zapped of their strength, especially spiritual strength. It is during these times that Christians must remember what God has to say, "be strong." When Joshua assumed the leadership position from Moses the message from God was to "be strong." Joshua would need strength for the battles ahead, but more importantly he would need strength of character. First, strength of character to obey God's law and secondly to be an example to God's people. You are no different from Joshua, because you too need strength especially spiritual strength to fight the spiritual battles in the present age.

Joshua was aware that he needed to "be strong" in his action for God. He was the leader, the man of action, so he had to demonstrate his strength. Christians are called to be men and women of action. Sometimes we get so involved that reality escapes us and we forget that our strength comes from God. The Apostle Peter was aware, as you should be, that Christians serve in the kingdom of God "by the strength which God supplies" (1 Peter 4:11).

God not only supplies strength to believe, but also the strength to continue to believe. God told Joshua to "Be strong and courageous! Do not tremble or be dismayed..." (Joshua 1:9). Why should Joshua's faith not be shaken? He had to get hundreds of thousands of people across the Jordan River during flood stage. The cities beyond the Jordan were fortified and what about all the problems associated with invading the enemy on his home ground. Joshua probably had good reason to tremble and be dismayed, because Joshua faced some major choices. The words God gave Joshua, "the Lord your God is with you," (Joshua 1:9) strengthened Joshua's faith so he could handle the transitions, whatever they may be. Have you had doubts since you became a Christian? I have! During my final year in seminary, academic endeavors just about swept me away. The various disciplines in critical thought were causing me to question the authority of Scripture. Frustrated and aware of the danger, I went to a professor and explained my quandary. He said, "no problem." I said, "big problem" because I was questioning the authority of Scripture and ultimately the authority of God. After a lengthy discussion he finally pointed out that I needed strength from God, not only to believe, but to continue in the faith. I did continue in the faith. The command from God was "Be strong and courageous! Do not tremble or be dismayed, for the Lord your God is with you wherever you go" (Joshua 1:9).

Sylvester Stallone was the protagonist in the movie "Lockup." He was unjustly imprisoned, so he tried to escape. During the escape plan, his partner told Stallone to turn left, but Stallone argued that he should go right. At his partner's insistence, he went left and the prison guards captured him. It turned out that his partner betrayed him and was an informer for the prison official. Making the wrong turn can be very painful.

God told Joshua not to make any turns. "Be careful to do according to all the law which Moses My servant commanded you; do not turn from it to the right or to the left..." (Joshua 1:7). Do not turn from the law, either to the right or to the left. One of the reasons Christians get frustrated during the transitions of life is a disregard for holding to the centrality of God's law. The New Testament cogently and convincingly explains the expectations of all Christians. "Be perfect, therefore, as your heavenly Father is perfect" (Matthew 5:48). Jesus said in another place "If you love me you will keep my commandments" (John 14:15). Guess where you get the strength to keep God's commandments? Yes, it comes from God. Christians receive and rest upon Christ alone for saving grace. God empowers Christians to believe and Christians will continue to believe as the Lord gives strength. Matthew explains it this way: "And she will bear a Son; and you shall call His name Jesus, for it is He who will save His people from their sins" (Matthew 1:21). Jesus will save His people and then He will enable them with strength to stay on the straight path and not turn either to the right or the left.

Christians often take a turn toward legalism. The word legalism may describe the meritorious necessity of keeping the law to earn salvation. Other times legalism defines a man-made moral code which allegedly binds all Christians. For our purposes legalism means that someone imposes an act of obedience that the Lord does not impose. For instance, some people teach that it is a sin to smoke cigarettes. It certainly is a nasty habit and may cause health problems, but the Bible does not address the subject. "You can't smoke, drink, dance or date girls that do" is an old cliché that describes legalism. Joshua was warned not to turn from the law of God either to the right or the left. Whatever direction legalism goes, do not make that turn. Jesus made his most scathing attack against the Pharisees. They were the legalist of His day. Avoid the wrong turn to legalism.

Christians have a tendency to go to the right or the left and the opposite of legalism is antinomianism. Hey, what a big word. Not really, just break it down. It comes from two Greek words, *anti* meaning "against" and *nomos* which refers to the "law of God." So an antinomian is against the law of God. This view drives the Christian away from the need to daily confess sins and vigorously follow the Lord. Oh, you say, I'd never be against the law of God. Pride may overcome us unless we ask the question: How is our obedience? Are we striving to keep every commandment or do we commit little acts of treason and just fail to acknowledge those acts? Maybe you don't commit adultery, but what about fantasy? Maybe you don't kill, but what about gossip? Maybe you don't steal, but what about envy or greed? Keeping the law of God is exacting and taxing of which no mere human being is able claim 100% success. Your responsibility is to be strong and courageous and to obey the God who created you.

God's power is demonstrated through His people. We see His power most evidently as we face choices throughout life. Joshua needed God's power to fight the battles necessary to conquer and settle in the land God promised to His people. You need God's power to conquer the evil forces that would try to captivate and control your life. The Israelites looked forward to settling in the Promised Land. You look forward to settling in the New Heavens and the New Earth. God's strength comes moment by moment, day by day, year by year. When you face that difficult choice, remember that your endurance is a demonstration of God's power in your life.

Your endurance is part of the process of being "strong and courageous." God's message to Joshua is as applicable to Christians today as it was to Joshua. God didn't fail Joshua and He will not fail you.

There are benefits associated with making godly choices. "This Book of the Law shall not depart from your mouth, but you shall meditate in it day and night, that you may observe to do according to all that is written in it. For then you will make your way prosperous, and then you will have good success" (Joshua 1:8).

A privilege is a right granted to someone. Joshua was privileged to receive God's promise and power to conquer and settle the Promised Land. Christians are the most privileged of all people. They too receive God's promise and power. The Christian is promised eternal life without fear or anxiety. Most of us look at choices in life with a fear of failure. I've presented the gospel in a nutshell many times only to hear these words. "I'm not going to accept Christ until I can live for Christ." It is the fear of failure that keeps many a person from making a transition. Transitions are privileges that come from God. Transitions are privileges because they anticipate a measure of success. "You will be prosperous and successful," so God said to Joshua. Prosperity and success can't be measured in dollars and cents. Prosperity and success is the peace and joy you experience as God gives you His promises and His power during the transitions of life.

Where do we go now, the lepers asked each other as they sat at the entrance gate of Samaria? There was a famine in the city and the enemy, the Army of the Arameans, camped outside the city to prepare for a siege against Samaria. If the lepers went into the city, they would probably die from hunger. Death was almost certain if they stayed at the city gate. They decided to go to the camp of the enemy, the Arameans. The lepers said "If they spare us, we shall live; and if they kill us, we shall but die." An astute observation? Not really, they just did not know where to go to survive. The balance of life hung in that transition for the lepers. (Read 2 Kings 7:1-16 for the biblical narrative). What transitions threaten you today? You have lost your job and the economic picture is so bleak you are unable to find work. You recently found out your life partner no longer loves you and wants to separate. You've just discovered you have a serious illness that may be life threatening. Your child has just announced that Christianity is not for him or her. A natural catastrophe (i.e. earthquake, tornado, flood, etc) has destroyed your earthly possessions. Or maybe your little girl, who is now 22 years old, wants to get married. The question is, Where do we go now? The answer is: Go to God. From the days of Joshua to the present time, God has not changed. The promises God made to Joshua are your promises. The power God gave to Joshua is your power. God's promises have never failed and His power is beyond human comprehension.

Escape from the lies of Satan. Forget the fantasy of Satan's deceptive world and step into the world of reality. Your perspective toward making godly choices will be radically changed when you learn and experience the reality of God's world from His Word. You will learn from His unchanging inspired Word to make godly choices.

14. Well Begun is not Enough

But the children of Israel committed a trespass regarding the accursed things, for Achan the son of Carmi, the son of Zabdi, the son of Zerah, of the tribe of Judah, took of the accursed things; so the anger of the LORD burned against the children of Israel.

Joshua 7:1

Richard Nixon was a man of many gifts and abilities. Zeal, enthusiasm, and hard work enhanced his political career and he made it to the top. Even with all his accomplishments, well begun was not enough. We're all like Richard Nixon in that our decisions should lead us closer toward the goal, whether the goal is to be president of the United States or a good husband or a faithful believer. The principles that guide the direction of progress toward a goal are the same for all classes of people. These principles transcend time and space. We, like the Apostle Paul, are challenged to "press on toward the goal for the prize."

God blessed the leadership of Joshua. Joshua's track record was excellent until he engaged in a little skirmish with the folk at Ai. The defeat at Ai was a transition for sure, but without the favor of God. "Why did this happen to me?" is a question we've all asked at one time or another. Joshua was a bit more pious, but fundamentally that was his question to God when Ai defeated Israel. The narrative in Joshua chapter seven has a literary style typical to Old Testament Hebrew. The chapter begins with a problem. "The anger of the Lord burned against the sons of Israel" (Joshua 7:1). The chapter ends with a solution. "The Lord turned from the fierceness of His anger" (Joshua 7:26). The verses in between explain through a series of smaller transitions how the Israelites made it through a major transition. The fundamental lesson in this chapter is that Christians must be aware of making ungodly choices.

A pastor friend vividly described an assault made against his character by someone in the congregation. I asked my friend if the person was a Christian. He laughed, as if I was asking a stupid question, and said, "he is an elder in the church." I responded by pointing out that my question had nothing to do with his office in the church. Sometimes we all forget that we're sinners. I simply wanted my pastor friend to admit that the elder was a sinner and the elder was not above making an ungodly choice. The pattern of sin has not changed since the fall of the human race. Eve saw the fruit. Eve lusted after the fruit. Eve took the fruit. King David, the apple of God's eye, saw the beautiful woman. King David lusted after the beautiful woman and he took the beautiful woman. An ungodly choice may spring from the rebellious sinful nature, so be prepared to identify the root of these sins. If you can identify the root of these sins, then you can acknowledge the sins and turn a sinful choice into a positive growing experience by asking forgiveness, repenting, and being reconciled according to biblical instruction.

God told the Israelites to "keep away from the devoted things, so that you will not bring about your own destruction..." (Joshua 6:18). The Israelites responded by acting "unfaithfully in regard to the devoted things" (Joshua 7:1). The "devoted things" in Jericho were detestable to God except for some metals that could be purified for the Lord's use. Achan sinned by stealing from the Lord. This sin involved a breech of the covenant to keep God's commandments. The continued success of the Israelites was contingent upon their faithfulness.

The unexpected fall is the most painful fall. Joshua and his company experienced the over throw of Jericho with astonishing success. Ai was smaller and less fortified than Jericho, yet the Israelites suffered a tremendous loss. After a successful win at Jericho, the response was "do not weary all the people for only a few men are there..." (Joshua7:3). Pride and arrogance seemed to overtake the Israelites. How quick the Israelites forgot God's grace and tried to replace God-power for man-power. A major victory or a time of prosperity for the Christian may be the most vulnerable for the sin of pride to raise its ugly head.

Unfaithfulness and pride will destroy Christians, if they fail to acknowledge the sins that result from ungodly choices. Achan's record of unfaithfulness and pride should be sufficient to teach us not to make the same mistake. Moving through the transitions of life is not easy. In the providence of God, there are hills and valleys in the Christian experience. There is a sense of unpredictable inconsistency in the Christian experience. When we are on a high, we think "we can do it" without God's grace (Joshua 7:3). No matter how good things look around us, unfaithfulness and pride may be hiding in the victory to deceive us. Acknowledge the sin of pride and pray for God's wisdom to make a godly choice.

Joshua was wise to identify the source of the sin as unfaithfulness and pride. Equally important was his reaction to these sins. Joshua responded to the defeat with a sense of anger. Joshua and the elders tore their clothes and put dust on their heads (Joshua 7:6-7). This symbolic act of sorrow and grief is followed by a question to the Lord. "Why did You bring us here to destroy us?" The fundamental idea is to blame God. The idea is a contradiction and the statement is a paradox. How can anyone blame a blameless God? Christians commit this act of treason and never think twice about it. When God confronted Adam for violating God's command, Adam said, "the woman you gave me, it's her fault." When God turned to the woman she said, "The serpent deceived me, it's his fault." The sinful nature looks for a way to cover up ungodly choices. When we sin we act like its God's fault. God slaps our hands; we blame God and then get angry because we've been accused. This brings on another, "Lord, why is this happening to me" reaction? The reaction should be, Lord, I acknowledge my sin, please forgive me.

Joshua and the Israelites were victims of Achan's sin. The twentieth century has ushered in the age of victimizationalism. The news media and talk show hosts spend a major part of their air time informing the public of a poor soul who was victimized by society. The victims accuse parents of child abuse. Employees charge employers with sexual abuse. One race charges the other with racial discrimination. The real troublemakers are the ones who are involved in litigation. The therapeutic agenda of modern psychology complicates the real issue known as sin. The remedy to these and other such problems will be found by acknowledging the sin of anger and asking God for forgiveness.

Joshua not only felt victimized, there was a sense of defeat and despair. "And Joshua said, 'Ah, Sovereign Lord, why did you ever bring this people across the Jordan to deliver us into the hands of the Amorites to destroy us?'" Joshua uses the interjection, Ah, but I'm not sure why he uses it. Interjections are used in most languages to express an emotion or to get attention. In English we use interjections like oh, hey, hello, yes or no. Joshua does not use the interjection, Ah, any other place. Other Old Testament authors used the word to express excitement or a sudden surprise. For instance, when Gideon saw the angel of the Lord he exclaimed, "Ah, Sovereign Lord! I have seen the Angel of the Lord face to face!" Was Joshua excited or did he just want to get the Lord's attention? Probably both! In any event, the context indicates that Joshua spoke from a state of confusion. When the whole world around us is falling apart and we are in the middle, we too cry out, "hey Lord, give me a break. I'm a victim of circumstances." For the Christian, defeat and despair is like an illusion. The circumstances are real, but they are temporary. God is in control.

Joshua calls on the "Sovereign Lord." The word "sovereign" is translated from the Hebrew word *adoni* and primarily refers to God, the creator and owner of the universe. It indicates the fullness of His majesty. Joshua also calls on the Lord, that is Jehovah, the personal God of Israel. Joshua did not need therapy. He didn't need to file a lawsuit to get even with the folk at Ai. Joshua made a godly choice. He called on God!

I arrived at the hospital to visit a friend diagnosed with lymphoma and brought with me a heavy heart for my friend. Instead of finding gloom and despair, the room was filled with hope and stability. After a brief visit, my friend said, "God does not make mistakes and this is happening for a reason." I was overwhelmed by the genuine expectation of God's mercy and grace. This dear Christian was able to resist the seductive nature of Satan and embrace the reality of God's presence. Your confidence in Christ will see you through the dark times of defeat and despair.

14. Well Begun is not Enough

Acknowledge your need and let your self-confidence become Christ-confidence.

Idol makers are not new or unique to this present generation. Idolatry is the act of devotion to the imaginary. To worship an idol means to give reverence to a fantasy or a spurious notion. Hollywood producers have exaggerated the limits of fantasy in the film making industry. They have lost touch with reality by creating illogical sequences and images of absurdity. I walked into the den to find Clint Eastwood playing on a movie depicting the good guy. He was driving a bus across town in an attempt to reach the courthouse to expose a bad guy. The police mounted a team to prevent Eastwood from making the trip. The large police force (it seemed like 1000's of policeman) used pistols and rifles to try and stop the bus. They must have shot tens of thousands of bullets in the bus. However, they never hit Eastwood or shot the tires on the bus. The movie was beyond fantasy. It was literally the impossible image. Achan allowed this type of idol making to control his thinking. Christians today are no less subject to fall into this trap.

The story of Achan's sin is a story about idol making or disgraceful devotions. Improper devotions toward "people" or "things" are not only disgraceful, they are dangerous. They are so dangerous that the Lord told Joshua that the Israelites could not stand against their enemies. For the Israelites the enemy was all the different tribes living in the land that was promised to the Israelites. The enemy for the Christian is just as real and just as powerful as the enemies of the Israelites. Christians must deal with the enemy which takes the form of cultural wars, disenchanted special interest groups, religious ideologies and a host of other perversions.

The appropriate response to ungodly choices is to consecrate yourselves in preparation for the Lord to help you through the dilemma. This means we have a sense of holiness toward God. The holiness of God denotes his majesty, purity, and dignity. It is important for Christians to reflect on God's character so they can see how far they are from God. Then Christians can begin to "consecrate themselves" (Joshua 7:13). The act of consecration means to "get your act together." My childhood was filled with playtime. Most children playing outside generally get dirty and sweaty and I was no exception. One day my dad told me we were having visitors for the evening meal. My first question was, "do I have to take a bath?" Not only did I have to take a bath, I had to wear nice clothes and stay clean. I consecrated myself so I would be presentable to our guests. As Christians, we need to present ourselves to the Lord after we have examined our lives and made proper preparation for the Lord's visit to us. This is the beginning of the process to get prepared to "stand against your enemies."

Preparation is not enough. The holiness of God demands confession. I have often wondered what would have happened if Adam had confessed his sin immediately to God. Read David's response in Psalm 51 when Nathan confronted David with his sin.

Have mercy upon me, O God,
According to Your lovingkindness;
According to the multitude of Your tender mercies,
Blot out my transgressions.
Wash me thoroughly from my iniquity,
And cleanse me from my sin.

For I acknowledge my transgressions,
And my sin is always before me.
Against You, You only, have I sinned,
And done this evil in Your sight—
That You may be found just when You speak,
And blameless when You judge.

Behold, I was brought forth in iniquity,
And in sin my mother conceived me.
Behold, You desire truth in the inward parts,
And in the hidden part You will make me to know wisdom.

Purge me with hyssop, and I shall be clean;
Wash me, and I shall be whiter than snow.
Make me hear joy and gladness,

That the bones You have broken may rejoice.
Hide Your face from my sins,
And blot out all my iniquities.

Create in me a clean heart, O God,
And renew a steadfast spirit within me.
Do not cast me away from Your presence,
And do not take Your Holy Spirit from me.

Restore to me the joy of Your salvation,
And uphold me by Your generous Spirit.
(Psalm 51:1-12)

If you are overtaken by sin and make an ungodly choice, cry out to God. Cry out to God for forgiveness, grace, peace, and joy.

We are living in the age of "rights." Such expressions as "I want to do my own thing" or "I've got to be me" are part of this individualistic revolution. Although Christians are not required to sin, they do sin. How should Christians respond to each other when ungodly choices result in sin. Christians are individual citizens in the kingdom of God, but not only individuals, they are a part of the larger community. In the New Testament there are about two dozen reciprocal commands (i.e. - love one another, pray for one another, etc.). The command to "bear one another's burdens" in Galatians 6:2 is often either ignored or misinterpreted. The context demands Christians to bear the burden of sin for other Christians. This, like other one another commands, indicates a community of believers. My sin is not just my sin. It is also your sin. A chain is no stronger than its weakest link. When the pressure is on then the weakest link will break and the whole chain is disabled. If the individual repair is made, the whole chain will be useful once again.

We live in an age when addiction, recovery, and co-dependency are the topics of talk shows, authors, and news media. Is addiction a real problem? Is recovery an important and necessary discipline for Christians to discuss? No, but confession of sin is important and necessary. What we forget are the solutions given to us by a sovereign God. Ungodly choices and sin go together. Inherent in these choices are dangers which require attention.

Well begun is not enough. It is not the beginning line of a race that counts. It is the finish line. During the race you will make ungodly choices. When you do, run to Jesus Christ. In Him you will find forgiveness and grace. When the race ends you will be able to say as Paul did, "I have finished the race, I have kept the faith."

15. Joseph's Godly Choice

Now Joseph had been taken down to Egypt. And Potiphar, an officer of Pharaoh, captain of the guard, an Egyptian, bought him from the Ishmaelites who had taken him down there. The LORD was with Joseph, and he was a successful man; and he was in the house of his master the Egyptian. And his master saw that the LORD was with him and that the LORD made all he did to prosper in his hand. So Joseph found favor in his sight, and served him. Then he made him overseer of his house, and all that he had he put under his authority. So it was, from the time that he had made him overseer of his house and all that he had, that the LORD blessed the Egyptian's house for Joseph's sake; and the blessing of the LORD was on all that he had in the house and in the field. Thus he left all that he had in Joseph's hand, and he did not know what he had except for the bread which he ate. Now Joseph was handsome in form and appearance.

(Genesis 39:1-6)

Joseph, the son of Jacob, was a man of wisdom, sensibility, patience, and self-control. Jacob loved Joseph. Jacob gave Joseph a special robe. It was probably a garment of distinction with sleeves, which implied special privileges. Joseph's brothers "hated him" because Jacob, "loved him more than all his brothers" (Genesis 37:4).

God revealed his plan to save His people through dreams. Joseph was the chosen man that God used to reveal His plan of salvation for Jacob and his descendents. Joseph's brothers hated him and "could not speak peaceably to him" (Genesis 37:4). Even his father "rebuked him" and although his brothers envied him, Jacob, "kept the matter in mind" (Genesis 37:11). Joseph was a type of Christ, because God used him to preserve the off-spring of Israel. Joseph was a special man with a special calling.

His brothers resented him and wanted to kill him. Reuben convinced his brothers not to outright kill Joseph, but instead put him in a pit. Later he was sold to some slave traders. Joseph was taken to Egypt and sold into slavery. Joseph had a unique relationship with God, but he was still a sinner. Like all sinners, Joseph would be confronted with trials and temptations. The reality of sin and responsibility before God demand constant attention. Retreat from sin is the message from Joseph. It is all about making godly choices.

The reality of sin is ever present, even for those whom God has called to Himself. Joseph became the "overseer" of Potiphar's household. The account of Joseph and Potiphar's wife reveals the reality of sin. Joseph was young and handsome in form and appearance (Genesis 39:6). Potiphar's wife lusted after Joseph. On three occasions Joseph was confronted with the reality of sin.

> And it came to pass after these things that his master's wife cast longing eyes on Joseph, and she said, "Lie with me" (Genesis 39:7).

> So it was, as she spoke to Joseph day by day, that he did not heed her, to lie with her or to be with her (Genesis 39:10).

> She caught him by his garment, saying, "Lie with me." But he left his garment in her hand, and fled and ran outside (Genesis 39:12).

"Lie with me" is an imperative verb. It requires action. The first "lie with me" was probably in the form of an invitation; a mild form of a command. The second "lie with me" was probably a demanding request. The third "lie with me" was an outright command. To put it another way, if you do not obey, you will suffer the consequences. This was a ravishing enticement to sin. The temptation to this young man strikes at the one aspect of the mind, will and emotions that was extremely vulnerable, a sexual offer. Joseph was young, maybe in his late teens or early twenties. What a tremendous temptation! How could Joseph resist an offer to satisfy Potiphar's wife, but also give him pleasure. Joseph responded with an extraordinary, but godly choice.

15. Joseph's Godly Choice

But he refused and said to his master's wife, "Look, my master does not know what is with me in the house, and he has committed all that he has to my hand. There is no one greater in this house than I, nor has he kept back anything from me but you, because you are his wife. How then can I do this great wickedness, and sin against God?" (Genesis 39:8-9)

Joseph understood the reality of sin. What is sin? Sin is doing something that God has forbidden or not doing something that God commanded. Then how did Joseph know that it was a sin to disrespect authority? Potiphar gave Joseph wide latitude over the estate, however Potiphar kept "his wife" for himself (Genesis 39:9). Joseph respected Potiphar's authority according to the fifth commandment, the law of authority. There is one twist in this event; God had not given the Ten Commandments. It is a simple inquiry, but one that must be answered. How did Joseph know to obey the Ten Commandments since they were not given and written in stone until 200 years later? Jacob was not a very good example for Joseph to pattern his life, because Jacob had extramarital affairs (Genesis 35:22). Joseph learned the rules for marriage and family, probably from oral instruction from his elders. God's rule was, "a man shall leave his father and mother and be joined to his wife, and they shall become one flesh" (Genesis 2:24). God ordained the sanctity of marriage by the covenant of creation. Therefore, Joseph knew Potiphar's wife was off-limits. However, that does not answer the question, "How did Joseph know that to lie with Potiphar's wife was a sin against God?" The answer to the question is in the book of Romans. The inspired Word of God explains how all rational creatures understand the law. Gentiles "by nature do the things in the law, these, although not having the law, are a law to themselves, who show the work of the law written in their hearts, their conscience also bearing witness…" (Romans 2:14-15). Therefore, Joseph understood that his unfaithfulness would be a "sin against God" (Genesis 39:9).

Joseph made a godly choice. He ran away from sin. Although he was not privy to New Testament doctrines, he obviously understood the principles taught in the New Testament. Life is full of trials. God's children face trials everyday. Paul's makes an acute charge about trials. "All who desire to live godly in Christ Jesus will be persecuted" (2 Timothy 2:12). James says to "count it all joy when you fall into various trials, knowing that the testing of your faith produces patience" (James 1:2). Entertaining trials will lead to temptations and temptations may lead, even the believer, to make an ungodly choice.

Joseph faced considerable trials. The outcome of the events is evidence that he resisted temptation. He did not blame Potiphar's wife and he certainly did not blame God. He simply left the possibility for temptation behind. He literally "fled and ran outside" leaving the temptation behind him. There is always a way of escape. Paul explains this principle. "No temptation has overtaken you except such as is common to man; but God is faithful, who will not allow you to be tempted beyond what you are able, but with the temptation will also make the way of escape, that you may be able to bear it" (1 Corinthians 10:13).

Joseph made a godly choice and ended up in prison (Genesis 39:20). After he ended up in prison he made a godly choice to make the best of it. Confidence in the providence of God is the mark of a man possessed by the Spirit of God. Joseph's life demonstrates his unwavering hope and confidence that God's choices are always godly choices.

The Lord was with Joseph (Genesis 39:2).

The Lord caused Joseph to prosper (Genesis 39:3).

The Lord blessed the Egyptian house for Joseph's sake (Genesis 39:5).

The Lord was with Joseph and showed him mercy (Genesis 39:21).

15. Joseph's Godly Choice

The Lord was with him; and whatever he did, the Lord made it prosper (Genesis 39:23).

The life and story of Joseph extends from Genesis chapter 37 to Genesis chapter 50, with one exception. Genesis chapter 38 is a brief disjunction to the account of Joseph.

Genesis chapter 37 introduces Joseph and his brothers and their hatred for Joseph. Genesis chapter 39 describes Joseph as a godly man making godly choices. In between chapter 37 and 39 is the story of Judah's ungodly choice to commit adultery. Joseph in one place making a godly choice and his brother Judah in another place making an ungodly choice.

This is a familiar story, maybe too familiar. Christians may overlook the application of God's truth in their own lives. It would be wise to put this story in the context of the original audience. The original recipients were, most likely, the Israelites in the wilderness. How would the text apply to them? They were on their way to the Promised Land. However, they needed to hear the story of Joseph's godly choices. The Israelites would also face trials, temptations, struggles, and difficulties. They too would have to make choices; either godly choices or ungodly choices.

New Testament Christians are on their way to the Promised Land, now known as the New Heavens and the New Earth. They must make choices. The first and most important choice is whether or not to have a favorable relationship with God through the Lord Jesus Christ by the power of the Holy Spirit. If you choose Christ then you will love His law and endeavor to make godly choices.

16. Natural Law is God's Law

For as many as have sinned without law will also perish without law, and as many as have sinned in the law will be judged by the law (for not the hearers of the law are just in the sight of God, but the doers of the law will be justified; for when Gentiles, who do not have the law, by nature do the things in the law, these, although not having the law, are a law to themselves, who show the work of the law written in their hearts, their conscience also bearing witness, and between themselves their thoughts accusing or else excusing them) in the day when God will judge the secrets of men by Jesus Christ, according to my gospel.

Romans 2:12-16

Many Christians deny that Romans 2:14 and 15 teaches natural law. Others argue against natural law from philosophical and theological formulations. One Christian theologian said, "natural law is based on an unbiblical epistemology." However, he also says, "I affirm that, though unregenerate sinners invariably know God and certain truths about Him and His Law, and indeed may know many truths about God, special revelation challenges, confronts, and undermines their fundamentally distorted natural theologies and natural codes."[1]

The question is not whether or not there is an epistemological *a priori* connected with the law of God. Epistemology refers to the inquiry into the source and value of knowledge. However, my concern is ontological. To put it another way, does natural law exist? The quality or the quantity of natural law as it really is, will be the subject of another inquiry.

The Bible says, "for when Gentiles, who do not have the law, by nature do the things in the law, these, although not having the law, are a law to themselves, who show the work of the law written in their hearts, their conscience also bearing witness, and

---

[1] Peter Leithart, "Premise," Vol. 3, No. 2, Feb 29, 1996.

between themselves their thoughts accusing or else excusing them " (Romans 2:14 and 15).

John Calvin makes a comment on this text that must be repeated over and over again. Calvin said: "All nations…have some notions of justice…which The Greeks call preconceptions, and which are implanted by nature in the hearts of men."[2] The *New King James Version* used "Gentiles" and Calvin says, "nations." The Greek word *ethnos* translated into English as "Gentiles" or "nations" is a plural noun in the Romans text. Paul's emphasis in his letter to the Romans has been either on the Jews or the *ethnos* (Gentiles or nations, plural), so the word "Gentile" or "nations" represents all people groups other than the Jews. John Calvin is one among many of God's servants who believed that the Bible teaches natural law. The rebirth of natural law in modern times has been attributed to the Roman Catholic Church. It is sad that we have to think in those terms because the church should not have to give rebirth to something that is plainly taught in Scripture. We must not think the concept of natural law was an invention of recent times. Our church fathers from the first century until now have acknowledged natural law, even if it is much despised today. Let me give you a few examples from the early history of the church.

> Tertullian (160 - 215) Time even the heathens observe, that, in obedience to the law of nature, they may render their own rights to the (different) ages. For their females they dispatch to their businesses from (the age of) twelve years, but the male from two years later; decreeing puberty (to consist) in years, not in espousals or nuptials. "House-wife" one is called, albeit a virgin, and "house-father," albeit a stripling. By us not even natural laws are observed; as if the God of nature were some other than ours! (Ante-

---

[2] John Calvin, *Calvin's Commentaries*, Vol. 19 (Grand Rapids, MI.: Baker Book House,) p. 96.

16. Natural Law is God's Law

Nicene Fathers, Volume IV, Part Fourth, On the Veiling of Virgins, Chap. 11)

St. Chrysostom (344-407) For this reason, here dismissing this subject; and having given to the laborious and studious an opportunity, by what has been said, of going over likewise the other parts of Creation; we shall now direct our discourse to another point which is itself also demonstrative of God's providence. What then is this second point? It is, that when God formed man, he implanted within him from the beginning a natural law. And what then was this natural law? He gave utterance to conscience within us; and made the knowledge of good things, and of those that are the contrary, to be self-taught. (*Concerning the Statutes*, Homily 12. p. 421)

The evidence for natural law is found in great abundance, apart from Scripture.

- From the heathen world - Plato and Aristotle made explicit reference to natural law.
- From the absurdity of no law.
- From the ontological argument - Something created creation. That something was God, therefore God is in control of His creation, because dependent beings must rely on an Independent Being for any source of order, authority, power, and morality.

Natural law is found in early Greek philosophical thought, it is found in Christian theological expressions, and it is found among heathen writers who make no claim to clarify its definition.

The church of all ages has acknowledged natural law. Sometimes referred to as the law of nature, natural law has come under attack by some theologians in the contemporary church. The concept of natural law found in Romans 2:14 and 15 demands our careful attention. It is necessary to clarify the meaning of the words "natural law" in the context of Romans chapter two.

Natural law is not natural revelation. Natural revelation is a term used to describe what theologians call general revelation. General revelation refers to the scope and content of God making Himself known. The scope is the whole world and the content is limited to natural theology. Natural theology is a concept that refers to the knowledge people have of God through general revelation.

Natural law is so ill defined today that the term itself must be scrutinized in its context. Natural law theories seem to find a home in reason or what is often called rationality. Many theologians associate natural law with rationalism. For instance, one theologian made this comment.

> Natural law in Christian theology traditionally refers to the inherent and universal structures of human existence which can be discerned by the unaided reason and which form the basis for judgments of conscience about the good and evil and which therefore make it possible to say that that right is the rational. (*A Handbook of Theological Terms*, by Van A. Harvey)

It will be fruitless to examine all the definitions of natural law used in recent times. Webster's definition is: "a principle or body of laws considered as derived from nature, right reason, or religion and ethically binding in human society." If we use that definition, it would require an explication beyond the scope of this inquiry. Furthermore it would demand inquiry into every philosophical and theological reference contained in that dictionary definition. This chapter is included to show the relationship of natural law to God's law.

There are so many different ways to define natural law that time will not permit inquiry into all the false claims in this study. For instance, St. Thomas Aquinas denies natural law in some sense, but refers to it as eternal law. Then how do we answer Romans 2:14 Aquinas asked? Aquinas answers his rhetorical question.

16. Natural Law is God's Law

I answer that, as we have stated above, law, being a rule and measure, can be in a person in two ways: in one way, as in him that rules and measures; in another way, as in that which is ruled and measured, since a thing is ruled and measured in so far as it partakes of the rule or measure. Therefore, since all things subject to divine providence are ruled and measured by the eternal law. . ., it is evident that all things partake in some way in the eternal law, in so far as, namely from its being imprinted on them, they derive their respective inclinations to their proper acts and ends... . Therefore it has a share of the eternal reason, whereby it has a natural inclination to its proper act and end; and this participation of the eternal law in the rational creatures is called the natural law.[3]

For my purpose I prefer to define natural law as God's natural way of defining reality. Natural law establishes the standard or the measure of ethics in reality. In other words it tells us what we ought not to do and what we ought to do. When natural man makes a decision to act one way or the other, then his action reflects his morality. For instance when an unbeliever becomes angry with another person, what restrains the unbeliever from murder. God's law, from God's word, says, "do not murder" and yet the unbeliever does not have the Word of God, but does not murder. Why did he keep God's law? Why does the unbeliever not commit adultery, steal, lie, or covet, even though he does not have the Word of God? There is an epistemological dimension to this whole debate. Knowledge is ultimately inseparable from reality. Then how does the unbeliever keep the law of God if he doesn't know the law of God? The answer must be that the law of God is a rational and complete system of natural laws implanted in the hearts of men. To say anything different is to deny the clear teaching of Scripture. The law of God was naturally implanted in the heart of Adam and Eve,

---

[3] Thomas Aquinas, *Summa Theologicia*, 618.

Cain and Abel, Noah and his sons, Abram, Joseph even before the law of God was written in stone. All these men of old depended on the law of God written in their hearts. Natural law was abundantly sufficient to condemn their sins and remind them of the excellent perfections of God's holiness and the need for salvation.

If the law of God was natural to Adam and his progeny, where did natural law come from? It comes from God. Man is in a state of moral dependency from the Independent Being that created him. It would be out of character for that Independent Being to allow the dependent being to self-destruct. If the Independent Being did not give the dependent being regulations to control his behavior, then the dependent being would not survive. To put it another way the dependent being would have no purpose for existence.

Now if you ask, "how did I arrive at that conclusion" I would say natural theology of course. We naturally know certain things about the nature and character of God. Dr. James Henley Thornwell said it best. "Natural theology is that knowledge of God and of human duty which is acquired from the light of nature, or from the principles of human reason, unassisted by a supernatural revelation"[4] This Presbyterian theologian understands that ethics are "acquired from the light of nature." Let me quote from another of God's servants. "If the light of Natural Theology makes us certain of anything, it assures us of these two facts, that God is a righteous ruler, and that we are transgressors."[5] It seems that those Presbyterian theologians thought carefully and critically about natural law as it is found in Romans 2:14,15.

If we know we are transgressors then we know we have violated the law of God. Even more significant is that all men know they have violated the law and they know it through the natural means God has appointed for all men or the supernatural means

---

[4] James Henley Thornwell, *Theological*, p. 31.
[5] R. L. Dabney, *The Practical Philosophy* (Harrisonburg, VA: Sprinkle Publications, 1984), p. 518.

God has appointed for His people. The inspired apostle Paul says, "Gentiles, who do not have the law, by nature do the things in the law" (*New King James Version*, Romans 2: 14). The *New American Standard* translates it this way: "Gentiles who do not have the Law do instinctively the things of the law." The *New English Bible* says, "When Gentiles who do not possess the law carry out its precepts by the light of nature, then, although they have no law, they are their own law, for they display the effect of the law inscribed on their hearts."

The light of nature sounds so familiar and it should because it is found often in the Westminster Confession of faith. The Westminster divines were not afraid of natural theology or natural law as it should be obvious in their frequent use of "the light of nature." The following examples from the *Westminster Confession of Faith* speak for themselves:

> Chapter I, of the Holy Scriptures (1.1) "the light of nature manifests the goodness, wisdom and power of God."
>
> Chapter X, of Effectual Calling (10.4) - Men cannot be saved "be they ever so diligent to frame their lives according to the light of nature."
>
> Chapter XXI, of Religious Worship and the Sabbath Day (21.1) – "The light of nature showeth that there is a God, who hath lordship and sovereignty over all."
>
> Chapter XXI, of Religious Worship and the Sabbath Day (21.1) – "As it is of the law of nature, that, in general, a due proportion of time be set apart for the worship of God."

Natural law whether it is called the light of nature or the law of nature is found in Romans 2:14 when the apostle uses the word "nature." The Greek noun *phusis*, translated "nature" in the English text (Romans 2:14) describes a native condition. *Phusis* refers to a natural condition or to natural characteristics. In some early Greek writings *phusis* referred to the product of nature. When we speak of nature we speak of particular characteristics which are natural. For instance, within humanity the nature of the male is distinguished from that of the female.

When the apostle Paul used the words "by nature" it seems to me to be unnatural to say there is no natural law. When unbelievers do the things of the law by nature, it seems natural to call it natural law. Natural men fashion their moral lives according the natural law written in their hearts. Supernatural men, those human beings who are new creatures in Christ, also have the law of God before them by means of the Bible and they desire to live according to its dictates. Natural man does not desire to live according to God's law. Natural man keeps the law because of self-interest, not because he loves the law maker.

For some reason or the other Christians today want to place natural law and the moral law of God antithetical to each other. If they mean that God's law cannot exist apart from God, they are correct. It is not conceivable that a dependent being can have existence, intelligence, or order without being under the absolute authority and power of an Independent Being.

The Bible refers to some things that are unnatural. "For this cause God gave them up unto vile affections: for even their women did change the natural use into that which is against nature" (Romans 1:26). It is against nature to do that which is against God's law. The only way to go against natural law is to suppress it, to which every man is endowed with the capability to suppress God's law to a greater or lesser degree. If they mean that God's law is not natural to the human race, as God has given it to the human race, the age-old question stares us in the face: how does man obtain the law? How do professing atheists keep the law?

The confusion and sometimes the contradiction are almost too much for the human mind. For instance, let me quote from the *Westminster Theological Journal*.

"To be sure, Reformed theology opposes any and all forms

of autonomous natural theology, including natural law."

"Morality is established directly by God through supernatural or special revelation."

"Just as every individual knows the true God, though not savingly, each person has the things of the law written upon his/her heart (Rom 1:18-2:16)."[6]

Some theologians call natural law by the term natural morality. Playing word games will not resolve this difficult dispute. The Bible makes it very clear that the unbelieving world (nations, notice the plural) has the moral law by nature.

In Romans chapter 2 verse 15 the English Bible (NKJV) says "They show the work of the law written in their hearts." The English word "show" is translated from the Greek word *endeiknumi* which as a law term meant to "inform against another party." It would not be exaggerating to say it means to prove. The action of the verb "show" or "prove" reflects an ongoing action. I should also mention that Paul's assertion reflects certainty in the factual assertion of his proof. It is so clear that Scripture says the moral law by nature is shown or proven in the lives of all people.

Paul used the terminology "written" on their hearts. God wrote the law on the tablets prepared by Moses (Exodus 34:1 and 34:28). Now we must ask what it means that the law of God is written on the heart. The word heart in the New Testament might refer to the one of several things. It could refer to the soul of man, but the heart may also simply refer to one aspect of the soul, such as the mind or the emotions. One theologian wrote, "the heart is always in Scripture the source of the instinctive feelings from which those impulses go forth which govern the exercise of the under-

---

[6] Mark Karlberg, "Covenant and Common Grace," *Westminster Theological Journal* 50 (Fall 1988): 323-337.

standing and will."[7] The soul of man is not an instinctive essence because God endows the souls of men with the power of reason. Man is fallen, a sinner and unable to please God, but man is still able to think and make decisions. It is not our rational inability that allows us to see our own ignorance and sinfulness. It is God's law written on the heart. As Dr. John Gerstner has so well said, "It is the moral, not the natural, image which was lost in the fall."[8] The heart of unbelieving man finds the moral law distasteful, but not because he does not know the law, but because his conscience and rational abilities still exist. Natural man has a natural law, but he hates the lawgiver. They hate God because of his perfect moral character.

That brings us to the work of the conscience. The Bible says the conscience "bearing witness" is an active force (Romans 2:15). Whether the conscience is conceptual or a component of the mind is a question for metaphysical inquiry. The mind and the conscience are not always the same thing in Scripture. Jonathan Edwards' comments on the conscience are worth mention.

> Conscience is a principle implanted in the heart of every man, and is as essential to his nature as the faculty of reason, for it is a natural and necessary attendant of that faculty. But the will of a wicked man is contrary to it, and inconsistent with it. They choose those things which they know to be evil, and ought not to be chosen; they choose that which their own reason tells them is unreasonable and vile, and unbecoming men, and justly provoking to their Maker, and contrary to the end for which they are made.[9]

The concept of self-awareness must be associated with the conscience.

---

[7] Frederick L. Godet, *Commentary on the Epistle to the Romans* (Grand Rapids MI: Zondervan Publishing House, 1956), p. 124.
[8] Gerstner, *Rational Biblical Theology*, Vol. 2, p. 352.
[9] Gerstner, *Rational Biblical Theology*, Vol. 2, p.245.

We cannot separate "self-awareness" from the mind or the will. In Rom. 2:15 the conscience indicates human responsibility associated with self-awareness. I've read one place or the other that "the conscience is the central self-awareness of the knowing mind and acting will."

The unbeliever's conscience bearing witness is not dissociated from "their thoughts accusing or else excusing them." The Greek word for "thoughts" is *logismos*. This word could legitimately be translated "reasoning." Apparently the conscience is influenced by the reasonings of the unregenerate unbeliever. Sometimes his conscience convicts him by the reasoning he employs in the process of carrying on some kind of intelligent process. There are other times that his conscience excuses him even when he is guilty of violating God's law. There is either a little voice inside saying "what you're doing is bad" or it may say "what you're doing is good" even though in reality it is bad. For sure, human beings should not trust their conscience, because it is still under the influence of sin. If Christians understand that "the law of God which we call the moral law is nothing else than a testimony of natural law and of that conscience which God has engraved upon the minds of men,"[10] then natural law and the moral law are the same.

For sure when Christians talk about natural law, they are not talking about any aspect of human law devised apart from the Word of God. Natural law comes from God's moral law and God's moral law is found in the Word of God.

The main objection to natural law is that man is a fallen creature. Since unregenerate man is only interested in self-interest, he is unable in any moral sense to obey God. I say that when a sinner obeys the law of God he does so because of his natural ability and not his moral ability. As a result God is displeased with any obedience on the part of the unregenerate man.

---

[10] John Calvin, *The Institutes of the Christian Religion*, 2 vols. (Philadelphia, PA: The Westminster Press, 1960), vol. 2, p. 1504.

I want to remind you that the law of God written on the hearts of all men evidences itself in one of two different ways.

- The conscience bearing witness
- The thoughts (reasoning) accusing or defending

Since the conscience is the central self-awareness of the knowing mind and the acting will, the conscience has its own distinct function. The question is whether or not the conscience can err? Will the conscience always act on the side of truth? Or does the conscience concern itself with moral decisions? We have to go back to the fall. What happened when Eve and Adam ate of the forbidden fruit? The *Westminster Confession of Faith* consults the full counsel of God to answer the question. "By this sin they fell from their original righteousness, and communion with God, and so became dead in sin, and wholly defiled in all the faculties and parts of soul and body."[11]

What does it mean that men are defiled in all the faculties and parts of soul and body? The *Westminster Confession of Faith* answers that question with precision and biblical accuracy. "After God had made all other creatures, he created man, male and female, with reasonable and immortal souls, endued with knowledge, righteousness, and true holiness after his own image having the law of God written in their hearts."[12]

Reason and morality are two essential aspects of the soul? Reason is concerned with the powers of the mind. The only question that remains is whether or not the mind was destroyed at the fall. Theologians use the terminology "noetic effect of sin" in reference to this question. To put it another way, how was the mind affected by the fall of man? We know for certain that the fall did not destroy the mind. The mind was defiled, but not destroyed.

---

[11] *Westminster Confession of Faith*, 6.2.
[12] Ibid., 4.2.

16. Natural Law is God's Law

The ability to function, make decisions and recognize God's law written on the heart is related to the works of the conscience. Now we come back to the question, can the conscience err? Will the conscience always act on the side of truth? Or does the conscience concern itself with moral decisions?

Since the conscience is the central self-awareness of the knowing sinful mind it may or may not be trusted to comprehend the truth of God's law. The will chooses according to its inclination at the time. The mind understands and the will acts according to its nature. The law of God written on the hearts of all men obligates them to an absolute and ultimate authority.

I hope you can better see the necessity for teaching the biblical views of that we call natural law. Without natural law Paul could not have said and would not have said, "therefore you are without excuse" (Romans 2:1). Paul's arguments are inescapably before us and we should present this inescapable truth to all men. This biblical doctrine will be a great help in defending the faith before unbelievers.

The Jews have the law written on tablets; The Gentiles have the law written on their hearts. Both are without excuse. Whether it is the law of nature or the law of the stones, or the eternal law, or the moral law, their consciences bear witness and their reasoning powers condemn those who are without Jesus Christ.

The approaching judgment of Christ must also be considered in light of this discussion on natural law. The apostle Paul remembers that the Psalmist said, "for he knoweth the secrets of the heart." Jesus said, "These people draw near to Me with their mouth And honor Me with their lips, But their heart is far from Me. And in vain they worship Me, teaching as doctrines the commandments of men" (Matthew 15:8). There are people who enumerate some of the good things that such and such person has done. Outward works are not a measure of how well one keeps the law of God. Outward works are spurious, occasional and even they are often tainted with obvious evil intentions. External works, pomp, pageantry and false proclamations will not deceive the righteous eye of God. These things will never replace truth and reality. Truth is the prerequisite for Christian apologetics. Reality will not hide from truth. All men, both Jews and Gentiles, will be judged by Christ as Christ himself said: For not even the Father judges anyone, but He has given all judgment to the Son (John 5:22)

Yes, Jesus Christ will judge the living and the dead to see if they have any interest in Him. If Christ does not find that righteousness, they shall perish and be condemned to everlasting punishment in Hell. This final judgment will reveal the secrets, motives, and principles that govern men. Everything will be brought to light. Nothing will be hidden because natural law demands that the wisest heathen be judged by the law of God.

17. Choose Spiritual Success

Good Teacher, what shall I do that I may inherit eternal life?" So Jesus said to him, "Why do you call Me good? No one is good but One, that is, God. You know the commandments: 'Do not commit adultery,' 'Do not murder,' 'Do not steal,' 'Do not bear false witness,' 'Do not defraud,' 'Honor your father and your mother.'" And he answered and said to Him, "Teacher, all these things I have kept from my youth." Then Jesus, looking at him, loved him, and said to him, "One thing you lack: Go your way, sell whatever you have and give to the poor, and you will have treasure in heaven; and come, take up the cross, and follow Me." But he was sad at this word, and went away sorrowful, for he had great possessions.

Mark 10:17-22

Have you ever heard anyone say, "I try to live by the Ten Commandments." Have you ever heard anyone say, "I try to live by the gospel?" There is a relationship between the law and the gospel. Theodore Beza, Calvin's successor at Geneva wrote:

> We divide this Word (Bible) into two principal parts or kinds: the one is called the "Law" and the other the "gospel." All the rest can be gathered under the one or the other of these two headings. What we call "Law" is a doctrine whose seed is written by nature in our hearts....What we call the "gospel" is a doctrine which is not at all in us by nature, by which is revealed from Heaven (Matthew16:17, John 1:13) and totally surpasses natural knowledge....For, with good reason, we can say that ignorance of this distinction between Law and Gospel is one of the principle sources of the abuses which corrupted and still corrupts Christianity . (*The Christian Faith*, 4.22)

Some professing Christians proudly proclaim "no law" because they allegedly live in an age of grace. Dr. Michael Horton, in his book *Beyond Culture Wars* said, "The law has been reduced in its terror, so the Gospel has been reduced in its liberating word of pardon and justification. Instead of the cross satisfying God's just sentence of wrath for our sins, it is now a demonstration of how much God thinks we are worth. The Law removed, the Gospel becomes a new law that is easier and user-friendly."

The distortion of the law and the gospel is at epidemic levels in the church today. As it was during the days when our Lord walked on earth, through the medieval period in Western Christianity and during this present dispensation, the law and the gospel are considered contrary to each other.

The biblical account of the young rich ruler in Mark chapter ten is a good example of a confused man. His understanding of the law was wrong. His unbelief relative to the gospel was wrong. The Mark text refers to "a man" (Mark 10:17). The collateral text in Luke refers to the man in terms of "a ruler" (Luke 18:18). The gospel of John used the same word to refer to Nicodemus (John 3:1). Nicodemus was "a ruler of the Jews," therefore a member of the most prestigious and significant religious body among the Jews.

The scene in Mark chapter ten reveals the normal pattern of Jesus teaching and preaching the gospel. Often misapplied, this text of Jesus confronting the young rich ruler with the law and the gospel ought to gain attention in the modern church. Keeping the law and obeying the gospel is a matter of making godly choices. Unfortunately, they are often measured according to successful Christian living.

Today success orientation is a major factor in every part of life. The passion for success in business, school, sports, or any other engagement in life is often the goal of life. A successful business and for that matter every temporal enterprise has no essential eternal value. Understanding the law and believing the gospel will have consequences, either good or bad. The body dies, but the soul remains, so spiritual success is ultimately all that counts.

The young rich ruler had a question about spiritual success. "As Jesus started on his way, a man ran up to him and fell on his knees before him. Good teacher, he asked, what must I do to inherit eternal life" (Mark 10:17). This man, the young rich ruler, in the contemporary church would be considered a prominent church leader. His approach, posture, and enthusiasm must not overshadow the appearance of humility. Jesus was "out on the road" which makes this a public scene. The man did not take Jesus aside to talk to Him privately. The man came running to Jesus. He was obviously seeking Christ. He came in haste! He took the appropriate position before God incarnate. His kneeling posture reflects, not only a sense of humility, but he worshipped Jesus Christ. It took courage and determination to make his request public. More important than any other action was making his request known. The grammar and syntax from the Greek indicates a vigorous question. It was not a simple inquiry. There was a sense of anxiety. The primary interest was on asking, but running and kneeling preceded the question. He took a humble position in public risking the possibility of embarrassment. His question was not about successful living or meeting psychological needs. This man had a spiritual need.

Requests for physical or temporal needs were typical in the life of the Lord Jesus Christ. These were physical needs like wine for a wedding (John 2:1-10). Throughout his ministry requests for healing seemed like an everyday need. There were occasional requests for Jesus to raise a person from the dead like the daughter of Jairus (Mark 5:22). Modern church members appear to be more concerned about physical healing than spiritual healing.

It is not sensible to forget the needs in this physical temporal world, but the real need is for an eternal favorable relationship with the Lord God almighty. The young rich ruler somehow identified Jesus Christ as the source of eternal life. He realized that Jesus was able to provide an eternal favorable relationship with God. His question was, "What must I do?" He was asking Jesus what he must do in the future to secure eternal life. To put it another way he wanted to know what future work would be required to be saved? Like many rational creatures, he did not think about what he was asking. One does not work for a gift. He expected the result of his work to produce an inheritance; "That I may inherit" equals the potential rather than receiving the promise of God's covenant.   Since the young rich ruler addressed Jesus as "good" Jesus wanted to know more about his motive. "Why do you call me good? No one is good except God alone" Mark 10:18). This verse has been interpreted a couple of different ways with many nuances in those interpretations.

1. A contrast between the absolute goodness of God and his own goodness subject to the growth and trial in the circumstances of the incarnation. I say no to this interpretation!

2. Jesus realizes that this man does not recognize him as God. The young rich ruler saw Jesus the man; an exceptionally good man. Notice the thought pattern:

>   You call me good - A man.
>   No one is good - Any man.
>   God is good - God alone.

This young ruler saw Jesus as a man and he treated Jesus as a man. An illustration of this principle may be found in this story. A visiting minister substituted for Henry W. Beecher. A large crowd learning that Beecher was not speaking moved toward the doors. The visiting preacher opening remarks were, "All who have come here today to worship Henry Beecher may now leave the Church. All who have come to worship God keep your seats."

Christians need to get their eyes off men and get them on Jesus. When Christians discover Jesus Christ as the source of eternal life it will eliminate:

>   Man centered worship - focus on feelings, etc.
>   All false worship.
>   Man centered evangelism – "I won so many..."
>   The temptation to idolize Christian leaders.
>   Misunderstanding the mission and ministry of the church.

17. Choose Spiritual Success

One important aspect to the question: "What must I do to inherit eternal life?" The answer is you do nothing; you simply have a right understanding of the law and obey the gospel. You simply trust Christ and what He has done for you. If the Holy Spirit enables you to believe the gospel, you will gladly endeavor to obey the law of God.

A correct understanding of the law of God is necessary for spiritual success. Apparently, Jesus wanted to see if this seeker understood the commandments of God. Jesus said, "You know the commandments: Do not murder, do not commit adultery, do not steal, do not give false testimony, do not defraud, honor your father, and mother" (Mark 10:19).

Those particular commandments, known as the second table of law, are relative to relationships Christians have with one another. Taken at face value, many Christians like the young rich ruler would say, "I make it a point to keep those commandments. I do not murder, commit adultery, steal, lie, and always honored my parents." If Christians believe that they keep those commandments they ought to carefully study the full counsel of God.

The young rich ruler told Jesus, "I have kept" these commandments from my youth (Mark 10:20). A tidbit of Greek grammar is important at this point. "I have kept" is in the middle voice that practically means, "I have kept the law for myself." He, the young rich ruler produced the action and enjoyed the results. He did not make mention of God's enabling grace for him to keep the commandments. Even a theological novice should say, "I've done my best." I have been told that Dr. John Gerstner would tell his seminary students who didn't do so well on an exam "You've never done your best." The implication and probably rightly so, we do enough to get by.

Jesus did not confront this young religious leader with the God first commands. "You shall love the Lord your God with all your heart, with all your soul, and with all your mind" (Matthew 22:37). Obviously, the young rich ruler along with the rest of the sinful human race could not positively affirm absolute obedience, neither outwardly or inwardly.

The teaching from the gospel of Mark is that the young rich ruler did not believe and therefore was unable to practice the law and obey the gospel. However, Jesus did not scorn the man. The Bible indicates, "Jesus looking at him, loved him" (Mark 10:21). The Greek word *emblepo* translated "looking" implies intensely looking. Jesus gazed at him staring at the person, who unlike many was seeking eternal life."

The text also indicates that Jesus loved the young rich ruler. The word "love" is so misused in the English language that it is virtually impossible to explain in this brief monograph. God loves all of his creation in a general sense. He loves some of His creation in a special sense. In this case it was God's love in a general sense. God loved him by providing air to breath, food to eat, etc. It was a general love of pity and compassion.

If Jesus thought in terms of temporal success, He would have been thinking that the seeker was young, successful business man, eager, aggressive, influential, and a community leader.

Maybe he was like Matthew who had many friends who needed to experience the wonderful grace of Jesus. These suggestions are tongue and cheek! Jesus didn't look for nor need successful people to accomplish His mission.

The Savior offered the gospel, and in this particular case, there were some explicit requirements for this man to join the company of Jesus. Jesus knew this man had not kept the commandments, so Jesus confronted him with one commandment explicitly; You shall not covet. Jesus also confronted him with one implied commandment; You shall have no other gods before me. Jesus worded it, simple and positive. "Sell all you possess, give to poor, and follow the Living God" (Mark 10:21). The inordinate lust for possessions is a violation of the tenth commandment; you shall not covet. Furthermore, the young rich ruler loved his possessions more than he loved god.

The law convicts people that they have sinned against the true and living God. The conviction ought to lead to confession of sin; then believing the gospel. The wonder of the law and grace of the gospel work together for the salvation of the soul. The gospel liberates the sinner from having to keep the law to earn salvation. Then obedience to the law will become the passion of the new man.

Not all the secular success this world has to offer equals spiritual success that is the result of God's saving grace. The story does not have a pleasant ending. After hearing his sin and hearing the gospel offer, we see response by the young rich ruler. "But he was sad at this word, and went away sorrowful, for he had great possessions" (Mark 10:22). The young rich ruler left the presence of God incarnate characterized by two words.

Sad - The Greek word *stugnazo* translated "sad" means to have a gloomy appearance. He was probably shocked by the words of Jesus.

Sorrowful - The Greek word *lupeo* translated "sorrowful" which literally means grieved or distressed

The order of events and the impact was: After he was shocked then he went away distressed. He left the presence of his Creator having great possessions. The word possession is more often used to describe property, which he may very well have inherited. Was this man successful? Yes, he had it together as long as he lived on this earth. He has his inheritance of land and riches.

Was this man successful? No! Based on the biblical account when he left this earth he did not have an eternal inheritance in the favorable presence of God. He will not be able to claim one inch of property in the New Heavens and New Earth.

Make a godly choice and trust Jesus Christ the Lord and Savior for a favorable eternal relationship with the Lord God almighty. Trust and obey for there is no other way!

About the Author

Martin Murphy has a B.A. in Bible from Columbia International University and Master of Divinity from Reformed Theological Seminary. Martin spent nearly thirty years in the class room, the pulpit, the lectern, the study, and the library. He now devotes most of his time consolidating academic and practical gains by writing Christian books. He is the author of fourteen Christian books. He and his wife Mary live in Dothan, Alabama.

The Church: First Thirty Years, 344 pages, ISBN 9780985618179, $15.95. This book is an exposition of the Book of Acts. It will help Christians understand the purpose, mission, and ministry of the church.

The Dominant Culture: Living in the Promised Land, 172 pages, ISBN 970991481118, $11.95. This book examines the culture of Israel during the period of the Judges. It explains how worldviews influence the church and it reveals biblical principles to help Christians learn how to live in the culture.

My Christian Apology, 98 pages, ISBN 9780984570874, $7.95. This book investigates the doctrine of Christian apologetics. It explains rational Christian apologetics.

The Essence of Christian Doctrine, 200 pages, ISBN 9780984570812, $12.95. This book was written so that pastors and laymen would have a quick reference to major biblical doctrines. Dr. Steve Brown says it was written, "with clarity and power about the verities of the Christian faith and in a way that makes a difference in how we live."

Return to the Lord, 130 pages, ISBN 9780984570805, $8.95. This book is an exposition of Hosea. The prophet speaks a message of repentance and hope. Hosea's prophetic message to Old Testament and New Testament congregations is, "you have broken God's covenant; return to the Lord." Dr. Richard Pratt said, "We need more correct and practical instruction in the prophetic books, and you have given us just that."

Theological Terms in Layman Language, 130 pages, ISBN 9780985618155, $8.95. This book was written so that simple words like faith or not so simple words like aseity are explained in plain language. Theological Terms in Layman Language is easy to read and designed for people who want a brief definition for theological terms. The terms are in layman friendly language.

The Present Truth, 164 pages, ISBN 9780983244172, $8.95. Each chapter examines a topic relative to the Christian life. Topics such as church, sin, anger, marriage, education and more.

Doctrine of Sound Words: Summary of Christian Theology, 423 pages, ISBN 9780991481125, $16.95. This is a book of Christian doctrine in topical format. It covers a wide range of theological topics such as, the triune God, creation, providence, sin, justification, repentance, Christian liberty, free will, marriage and divorce, Christian fellowship, et al). There are thirty three topics beginning with "Holy Scriptures" and ending with "The Last Judgment." It is a systematic theology for laymen based on the full counsel of God.

Friendship: The Joy of Relationships, ISBN 9780986405518, 48 pages, $6.49. This is the kind of book that friends give each other and share the principles with each other. If friends do not feel comfortable sharing these relationship principles with each other, the friendship may not really exist. Friendship involves a relationship of distinction. It is a relationship that respects the dignity of another person. The Bible teaches a different version of what it means to be a friend than the popular culture teaches. There are many occasions when friends say they are friends, but they are not friends. "Even my own familiar friend in whom I trusted, who ate my bread, has lifted up his heel against me" (Psalm 41:9). A true friend will endure and sacrifice for a friend. "A friend loves at all times" (Proverbs 17:7) and "there is a friend who sticks closer than a brother" (Proverbs 18:24).

Ultimate Authority for the Soul, ISBN 9780986405501, 151 pages, $9.99. What is the ultimate authority for human beings? This book examines that question and concludes that every rational being has some recognition of God as the ultimate authority. Although God is the ultimate authority, He confers His authority by means of the Word of God. The author examines Psalm 119 to build a defense for the ultimate authority for the soul. Although this book was written for Christians, the author builds the case that authority is a principle necessary to maintain sanity and order in the family, the church and civil society. The Word of God connects the soul with reality.